The Australian **Womens**
Weekly
home library

THE
CHRISTMAS
BOOK

The publishers would like to thank the following contributors:

Maria Ragan, for "Bright and Simple" tree decorations on pp. 52–57, and "Country Christmas" decorations on pp. 58–61; Lynda Maker for Easy Garland on p. 62, Table Centrepiece on p. 64; Citrus Wreath on p. 66, Santas and Carollers on p. 68, Boxed Crackers on p. 78, Tags on p. 88, Potato Stamp Wrappings on p. 90, and wrapping papers on pp. 92 and 93; Janene Nicholls for Dave and Celeste on p. 70; Pam Worsdall for Stencilled Placemats on p. 74, Holly Tablecloth on p. 76, Stencilled Giftwrap and Carry Bags on p. 90, Etched Cards on p. 94, and Stained Glass Cards on p. 95; Yolanda Gifford for Appliqué Stockings on p. 82; Sandy Cull for Trims on p. 88; Jennie Beecroft of Beeline Products for Pressed Flower Cards on p. 96; Rosemarie Jeffers-Palmer of Artwise – The Amazing Paper Shop, Enmore, NSW, for Ribbon Cards on p. 97.

Microfleur flower presses are available from Beeline Products Pty Ltd,
PO Box 1837, Caboolture, Qld 4510, ph (07) 5498 5016.

HOME LIBRARY STAFF
EDITOR-IN-CHIEF: Mary Coleman
MANAGING EDITOR: Georgina Bitcon
FOOD EDITOR: Pamela Clark
ASSOCIATE FOOD EDITOR: Karen Hammial
PROJECT EDITORS: Liz Neate and Karen Green
SUB-EDITOR: Julie Collard
ART DIRECTOR: Alison Windmill
DESIGNER: Caryl Wiggins
STUDIO MANAGER: Caryl Wiggins
EDITORIAL COORDINATORS: Fiona Lambrou, Debbie Quick
MARKETING MANAGER: Nicole Pizanis

CHIEF EXECUTIVE OFFICER: John Alexander
GROUP PUBLISHER: Paul Dykzeul

PHOTOGRAPHERS: Andrew Elton, Joe Filshie, Andre Martin
CRAFT STYLISTS: Louise Owens, Georgina Dolling
ILLUSTRATOR: Jo McComiskey
PATTERN SHEET: Ficope Graphic Services

PRODUCED BY
The Australian Women's Weekly Home Library.
COLOUR SEPARATIONS BY
ACP Colour Graphics Pty Ltd, Sydney.
PRINTING BY
Times Printers Pte Limited

PUBLISHED BY
ACP Publishing Pty Limited,
54 Park St, Sydney; GPO Box 4088, Sydney, NSW 1028.
Ph: (02) 9282 8618 Fax: (02) 9267 9438.
email: AWWHomeLib@publishing.acp.com.au
http://awwhomelibrary.ninemsn.com.au
AUSTRALIA:
Distributed by Network Distribution Company,
GPO Box 4088, Sydney, NSW 1028.
Ph: (02) 9282 8777 Fax: (02) 9264 3278.
UNITED KINGDOM:
Distributed in the UK by Australian Consolidated Press (UK),
Moulton Park Business Centre, Red House Rd, Moulton Park,
Northampton, NN3 6AQ, Ph: (01604) 497 531, Fax: (01604) 497 533
email: Acpukltd@aol.com.
CANADA:
Distributed in Canada by Whitecap Books Ltd,
351 Lynn Ave, North Vancouver, BC, V7J 2C4, Ph: (604) 980 9852.
NEW ZEALAND:
Distributed in New Zealand by Netlink Distribution Company,
17B Hargreaves St, Level 5, College Hill, Auckland 1, Ph: (9) 302 7616.
SOUTH AFRICA:
Distributed in South Africa by PSD Promotions (Pty) Ltd,
PO Box 1175, Isando 1600, SA, Ph: (011) 392 6065.

The Christmas Book.
Includes index.
ISBN 1 86396 104 6.
1. Christmas decorations. 2. Christmas cookery. 3. Handicraft. 4. Carols, English.
(Series: Australian Women's Weekly Home Library.)
641.568

© ACP Publishing Pty Limited 1999
ACN 053 273 546

Cover: Christmas Pudding with Homemade Citrus Peel, page 24.

Contents

Festive Fare

Christmas dinner is the high-
light of the seasonal festivities,
and here we provide all the
right ingredients. You might
not find the traditional boar's
head and fattened goose, but
you will find a glazed ham
and roast turkey ... along
with a host of other roasts, a
delicious seafood platter,
puddings, cakes and sweet
treats — it's a recipe for the
best Christmas ever.

Nibbles

CHILLI CAPSICUM DIP WITH FOCACCIA STICKS

MAKES ABOUT 1¾ CUPS DIP AND 60 STICKS

Focaccia, the dense Italian bread available from some delicatessens, is a good partner for this dip, but substitutes like crackers or toast also work well. Dip can be made 3 days ahead, and kept, covered, in the refrigerator. Focaccia sticks can be made a day ahead; store in airtight container.

2 small (300g) red capsicums
¼ cup (60ml) lime juice
1 cup (70g) stale breadcrumbs
2 small fresh red chillies, seeded, chopped
4 cloves garlic, chopped
1 small (100g) red onion, chopped

FOCACCIA STICKS
16cm x 22cm piece focaccia
¾ cup (180ml) olive oil
1 teaspoon cracked black pepper
1 teaspoon garlic salt
1 tablespoon dried basil leaves

Quarter capsicums, remove seeds and membranes. Grill capsicums, skin-side up, until skin blisters and blackens. Cover capsicum pieces in plastic or paper for 5 minutes, peel away skin; chop capsicum. Blend or process capsicum with remaining ingredients until smooth. Serve with Focaccia Sticks.

Focaccia Sticks Split focaccia in half, cut each half into 3 pieces; cut each piece into 10 sticks. Brush top and sides of each stick with oil; sprinkle with combined pepper, salt and basil. Place on oven trays in single layer. Bake, uncovered, in moderately hot oven about 25 minutes or until browned and crisp.

SMOKED SALMON AND CAPER PIZZAS

MAKES 32

Commercially available butter puff pastry is a boon for busy cooks. Bases can be made a week ahead and stored in an airtight container.

2 sheets ready-rolled butter puff pastry
1 cup (200g) ricotta cheese
3 teaspoons hot water
2 tablespoons chopped fresh chives
3 teaspoons horseradish cream
6 slices (180g) smoked salmon, chopped
2 tablespoons drained capers
6 sprigs dill

Cut pastry into sixteen 5.5cm rounds; place on greased oven trays. Bake in very hot oven about 8 minutes, or until browned; cool. Split rounds in half. Combine ricotta and water in medium bowl; stir in chives and cream. Just before serving, spread ricotta mixture over rounds; top with salmon, capers and dill sprigs.

Both the chilli capsicum dip, left top, and the pizza bases can be made in advance of a party. To preserve the fresh delicacy of the pastry, the smoked salmon pizza topping, left below, is best added just before the guests arrive.

CAJUN POTATO WEDGES

MAKES ABOUT 2 CUPS EACH SAUCE
AND 64 WEDGES

While these popular wedges can be prepared in advance, they are best baked just before serving. Dipping sauces can be made a day ahead; keep refrigerated.

8 medium (1.6kg) potatoes
1/4 cup (60ml) olive oil
90g butter, melted
2 tablespoons ground cumin
2 tablespoons Cajun seasoning

PESTO DIPPING SAUCE
300ml sour cream
1/4 cup (60ml) bottled pesto
1/4 cup (20g) grated parmesan cheese

SWEET CHILLI DIPPING SAUCE
1/3 cup (80ml) mild sweet chilli sauce
300ml sour cream

Cut unpeeled potatoes in half, cut each half into 4 wedges. Boil, steam or microwave potatoes until just tender; drain, cool. Combine oil, butter and spices in large bowl; add wedges in batches, coat evenly with spice mixture. Place wedges on oven trays. Bake in hot oven about 45 minutes, or until crisp. Serve with Dipping Sauces.

Pesto Dipping Sauce Combine all ingredients in medium bowl; mix well.

Sweet Chilli Dipping Sauce Combine all ingredients in medium bowl; mix well.

CHILLI CASHEWS AND WALNUTS

MAKES ABOUT 3 CUPS

Recipe can be made 1 month ahead; store in airtight container in refrigerator.

1 1/2 cups (225g) unsalted roasted cashews
1 1/2 cups (150g) walnuts
2 teaspoons grated fresh garlic
1 1/2 tablespoons mild sweet chilli sauce
1 tablespoon soy sauce

Combine all ingredients in large bowl. Spread mixture on greased oven tray. Bake, uncovered, in moderate oven, stirring occasionally, about 20 minutes or until crunchy; cool.

BOCCONCINI AND TOMATO BRUSCHETTA

MAKES 20

Baby bocconcini, also known as milk cherries, are small balls of fresh mozzarella sold in whey. If unavailable, substitute ordinary bocconcini. Bruschetta is best if assembled close to serving.

40cm French bread stick
2 cloves garlic, peeled, halved
1/4 cup (60ml) olive oil
1/4 cup firmly packed fresh basil leaves
100g baby bocconcini, sliced
125g cherry tomatoes, sliced
Cracked black pepper

Trim ends from bread stick, cut bread stick into 2cm slices. Grill or toast bread both sides until browned lightly. Rub garlic over one side of each piece of toast; brush lightly with some oil. Top toasts with basil leaves, bocconcini and tomatoes. Drizzle with remaining oil. Sprinkle with cracked black pepper.

Bocconcini and tomato bruschetta, above, is as sensationally flavoursome as it is colourful. Two party favourites, chilli cashews and walnuts, and cajun potato wedges, left.

Main Courses

Poultry

ROAST TURKEY
WITH PORT GRAVY

SERVES 10

We have given three methods for roasting a turkey: the traditional method; a long slow method which results in a turkey to melt in your mouth; and, for those who want to cook outdoors, a delicious barbecue method. The choice is yours as is the choice of flavours used for seasoning (see pages 10–11). Fill both turkey cavities just before cooking. If you prefer not to cook the seasoning in the turkey itself, it can be cooked in oiled muffin pans, loaf pans or shaped into a loaf then wrapped in foil. This can be baked next to the turkey for about 30 minutes to one hour, depending on the quantity. Seasoning can be made a day ahead, cooled and stored, covered, in the refrigerator.

4kg turkey
2 tablespoons vegetable oil
2 tablespoons plain flour
1/4 cup (60ml) chicken stock
1/2 cup (125ml) port
2 tablespoons brown sugar

SEASONING
2 tablespoons vegetable oil
2 medium (300g) onions, sliced
500g sausage mince
4 cups (280g) stale breadcrumbs
2 tablespoons chopped fresh sage
**1/2 cup (60g) chopped walnuts
    or pecans**

Discard neck and giblets from turkey. Rinse turkey under cold water; pat dry inside and out. If filling the turkey, spoon the seasoning loosely into the cavities; sew up the cavities or close them using trussing skewers or toothpicks and kitchen string.

TRADITIONAL METHOD Place the turkey into oiled flameproof baking dish. Bake, uncovered, in moderate oven about 2¹/2 hours, or until turkey is tender, basting every 20 minutes with juices (cover turkey breast and legs with foil after 1 hour to prevent overbrowning). Remove turkey from dish, cover with foil to keep warm. Strain juices from dish into jug; remove fat from juices. Heat oil in same baking dish, stir in flour; stir over heat until well browned. Remove from heat, gradually stir in combined reserved juices, stock, port and sugar. Stir over heat until gravy boils and thickens; strain.

SLOW-COOK METHOD Place turkey into oiled flameproof baking dish; pour stock and half the port into dish. Cover tightly with greased foil. Bake in slow oven for 5¹/2 hours. Remove foil; brush turkey with combined remaining port and sugar. Increase temperature to moderate; bake, uncovered, 30 minutes or until turkey is well browned. Remove turkey from dish, cover with foil to keep warm. Strain juices from dish into jug; remove fat from juices. You will need 3 cups (750ml) juices. Heat oil in same baking dish, stir in flour; stir over heat until well browned. Remove from heat, gradually stir in reserved pan juices; stir over heat until gravy boils and thickens; strain.

BARBECUE METHOD If you cook the turkey on a barbecue rack, you will not be able to make the gravy at the end of cooking. If you wish to cook in the barbecue and still want gravy, use a disposable baking dish and finish the gravy on the stove. Place turkey on a roasting rack or basket, or in a disposable baking dish. Cook in covered barbecue, using indirect heat and following the manufacturer's instructions, about 2¹/2 hours, or until turkey is tender. If making the gravy, continue as for Traditional Method.

SEASONING Heat oil in large pan, add onion; cook, stirring, until onion is soft; remove from heat. Stir in remaining ingredients; mix well.

Serve roast turkey with seasoning and port gravy, made in the baking dish after the turkey is cooked.

How To Season a Turkey

1

Tuck wings under body.

2

Reserve 1 cup seasoning. Spoon remaining seasoning loosely into main cavity of turkey.

3

Secure opening with toothpicks.

4

Fill the space under skin at neck with reserved seasoning; trim skin and tuck under turkey. Secure with toothpicks.

5

Using kitchen string, tie the crossed legs together securely.

seasonings

PRUNE AND PISTACHIO SEASONING

1 tablespoon vegetable oil
1 large (200g) onion, chopped finely
4 cups (280g) stale breadcrumbs
1 cup (150g) shelled pistachios, toasted, chopped
1 cup (170g) seeded prunes, chopped
½ cup (125ml) cranberry sauce
2 tablespoons port
2 tablespoons chopped fresh flat-leaf parsley
2 teaspoons chopped fresh thyme
2 teaspoons chopped fresh sage
1 egg, beaten lightly

Heat oil in large pan, add onion, cook, stirring, until onion is soft; remove from heat. Stir in remaining ingredients; mix well.

ROSEMARY AND MUSHROOM SEASONING

Green onions are also known as scallions or small spring onions.

60g butter
10 green onions, chopped
4 bacon rashers, chopped
250g mushrooms, chopped finely
2 cups (140g) stale breadcrumbs
1½ tablespoons chopped fresh rosemary

Heat butter in large pan, add onion and bacon, cook, stirring, until onion is soft. Add mushrooms, cook 1 minute; remove pan from heat. Stir in remaining ingredients; mix well.

LIME SEASONING

Coriander is also known as cilantro or Chinese parsley.

30g butter
1 medium (150g) onion, chopped finely
2 cloves garlic, crushed
1 teaspoon grated lime rind
1½ tablespoons lime juice
¼ cup (35g) slivered almonds, toasted
2 tablespoons chopped fresh coriander leaves
1 cup (200g) cooked white long-grain rice

Heat butter in large pan, add onion and garlic, cook, stirring, until onion is soft; remove from heat. Stir in remaining ingredients; mix well.

POTATO, ROSEMARY, GARLIC SEASONING

90g butter
1 large (200g) onion, chopped finely
2 cloves garlic, crushed
1 teaspoon chopped fresh rosemary
5 medium (1kg) potatoes, chopped
¼ cup chopped fresh parsley
2 egg yolks
½ cup (40g) grated parmesan cheese
2 cups (140g) stale breadcrumbs

Heat butter in large pan, add onion, garlic and rosemary, cook, stirring, until onion is soft; remove from heat. Boil, steam, or microwave potatoes until soft, drain well; mash. Add potato to onion mixture with remaining ingredients; mix well.

SAGE AND ONION SEASONING

Packaged hazelnut (filbert) meal is available from supermarkets and health food stores.

30g butter
1 large (200g) onion, chopped
2 sticks (140g) celery, chopped
3 bacon rashers, chopped
300g sausage mince
2½ cups (175g) stale breadcrumbs
1 tablespoon chopped fresh sage
⅓ cup (35g) hazelnut meal
2 eggs, beaten lightly

Heat butter in large pan, add onion, celery and bacon, cook, stirring until onion is soft. Add mince, cook, stirring, until changed in colour. Remove from heat; cool. Stir in remaining ingredients; mix well.

PESTO SEASONING

30g butter
1 tablespoon olive oil
2 tablespoons pine nuts
2 cloves garlic, crushed
4 cups (280g) stale breadcrumbs
½ cup chopped fresh basil leaves
¼ cup (20g) grated parmesan cheese
2 eggs, beaten lightly

Heat butter and oil in large pan, add nuts, cook, stirring, until browned lightly; remove from heat. Stir in remaining ingredients; mix well.

FRUITY MINTED SEASONING

Hazelnuts are also known as filberts.

3 cups (210g) stale breadcrumbs
½ cup (60g) chopped
    roasted hazelnuts
¼ cup (40g) sultanas
¼ cup (35g) chopped dried apricots
¼ cup (20g) chopped dried apples
¼ cup (50g) seeded chopped prunes
6 green onions, chopped
2 tablespoons chopped fresh
    mint leaves
2 eggs, beaten lightly
2 tablespoons port

Combine all ingredients in large bowl; mix well.

ORANGE WATERCRESS
SEASONING

60g butter
1 medium (150g) onion, chopped
2 bacon rashers, chopped
350g watercress, chopped
2 cups (140g) stale breadcrumbs
2 tablespoons grated orange rind
⅔ cup (160ml) orange juice

Heat butter in large pan, add onion and bacon, cook, stirring, until onion is soft; remove from heat. Stir in remaining ingredients; mix well.

RICE AND PECAN SEASONING

3 cups (600g) cooked white
    long-grain rice
250g sausage mince
1 small (80g) onion, chopped
1 stick (70g) celery, chopped
½ cup (50g) pecans or
    walnuts, chopped
1 clove garlic, crushed
1 egg, beaten lightly
2 teaspoons dried mixed herbs

Combine all ingredients in large bowl; mix well.

FRUITY NUT SEASONING

Green onions are also known as scallions or small spring onions.

30g butter
1 medium (150g) onion, chopped
4 green onions, chopped
250g minced chicken
3 cups (210g) stale breadcrumbs
½ cup (60g) chopped
    roasted hazelnuts
1 egg, beaten lightly
2 tablespoons port
½ cup (75g) chopped dried apricots
1 teaspoon chicken stock powder
½ cup chopped fresh chives

Heat butter in large pan, add onion, cook, stirring, until onion is soft; remove from heat. Stir in remaining ingredients; mix well.

APRICOT AND WATER
CHESTNUT SEASONING

60g butter
1 medium (150g) onion, chopped
6 green onions, chopped
2 cloves garlic, crushed
4 cups (800g) cooked white
    long-grain rice
280g can water chestnuts,
    drained, chopped
2 sticks (140g) celery, chopped
⅓ cup (50g) chopped dried apricots
½ cup (35g) stale breadcrumbs
1 egg, beaten lightly
2 tablespoons chopped fresh parsley

Heat butter in large pan, add onions and garlic, cook, stirring, until onions are soft; remove from heat. Stir in remaining ingredients; mix well.

SPINACH AND
PINE NUT SEASONING

3 bacon rashers, chopped
1 clove garlic, crushed
1 medium (150g) onion, chopped
4 cups (800g) cooked white
    long-grain rice
250g packet frozen finely
    chopped spinach
1 tablespoon pine nuts, toasted

Heat a large non-stick pan, add bacon, onion and garlic, cook, stirring, until onion is soft. Add thawed spinach, cook until liquid evaporates. Remove from heat, stir in remaining ingredients; mix well.

HOW TO CARVE A TURKEY

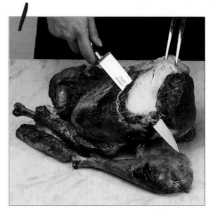

Remove wing, then thigh and drumstick on one side by cutting through thigh bone at joint where it joins body. Turn bird on its side; place cut-off wing, thigh and drumstick under bird to keep it stable. Carve across breast at top so slices incorporate some of seasoning.

Carve breast at other end.

Carve thigh and separate it from drumstick. Incorporate this meat with breast meat. Turn bird over and carve other side in same way.

TRADITIONAL ROAST CHICKEN

SERVES 6

While seasoning can be prepared a day ahead, fill the cavity of the chicken just before cooking. Any of the turkey seasonings can be halved and used for roast chicken.

1.5kg chicken
30g butter, melted
2 tablespoons plain flour
2 cups (500ml) chicken stock

SEASONING
1 medium (150g) onion, chopped
1 cup (70g) stale breadcrumbs
1 egg, beaten lightly
2 bacon rashers, chopped
2 tablespoons chopped fresh parsley
½ teaspoon dried thyme leaves

Remove excess fat from chicken. Rinse chicken under cold water; pat dry inside and out, tuck wings under body. Spoon Seasoning loosely into cavity; secure with toothpicks. Using kitchen string, tie legs together securely.

Place chicken, breast side up, on wire rack in baking dish, brush with butter. Bake, uncovered, in moderate oven about 1½ hours, or until well browned and tender. Place chicken on serving plate; keep warm.

Drain all but 2 tablespoons of juices from baking dish, stir in flour, stir over heat until bubbling and browned lightly. Remove from heat, gradually stir in stock, stir over heat until gravy boils and thickens. Serve chicken and seasoning with gravy.

Seasoning Combine all ingredients in medium bowl; mix well.

Traditional roast chicken is crispier and less fatty when cooked on a wire rack that is positioned in a baking dish.

DUCK WITH CHERRY SAUCE

SERVES 4

*Seasoning can be prepared a day ahead.
Fill cavity of duck with seasoning
just before cooking.*

425g can sweet red cherries
15g butter
1 clove garlic, crushed
2 tablespoons slivered almonds
2 teaspoons grated orange rind
1/4 teaspoon ground cumin
**3 cups (210g) stale white
    breadcrumbs**
1 egg, beaten lightly
1 tablespoon orange juice
1.6kg duck

CHERRY SAUCE
3 teaspoons cornflour
1/2 teaspoon sugar
1/4 cup (60ml) orange juice
1 chicken stock cube

Drain cherries, reserve syrup and half the cherries for sauce. Cut remaining cherries into halves. Heat butter in large pan, add garlic, almonds, rind and cumin, cook, stirring, until almonds are browned lightly; remove from heat. Stir in halved cherries, crumbs, egg and orange juice; mix well.

Rinse duck under cold water; pat dry inside and out. Spoon seasoning loosely into cavity. Using kitchen string, tie legs together securely (wings not tucked in).

Place duck, breast-side up in a baking dish. Bake, uncovered, in moderate oven for about 1 1/2 hours. Serve duck and seasoning with Cherry Sauce.

Cherry Sauce Blend cornflour and sugar with orange juice in medium pan, stir in crumbled stock cube, reserved cherries and syrup; cook, stirring until sauce boils and thickens.

Duck cooked with a seasoning of cherries, almonds and orange rind and served with cherry sauce.

Pork

PORK WITH APPLES AND CARAMELISED ONION JAM

SERVES 8

Ask the butcher to score the rind and tie the loin of pork. Pork and apples (we used Granny Smith apples for this recipe) are best cooked close to serving time. Caramelised onion jam can be made 3 days ahead and kept, covered, under refrigeration.

2.5kg boned, rolled loin of pork
2 tablespoons olive oil
2 teaspoons salt
8 small (1.2kg) green-skinned apples
16 seeded prunes
8 small sprigs fresh rosemary

CARAMELISED ONION JAM
30g butter
4 large (800g) onions, sliced
2/3 cup (130g) firmly packed brown sugar
1/2 cup (125ml) brown malt vinegar
1 teaspoon finely chopped fresh rosemary

Place pork on wire rack in baking dish; rub oil and salt into rind. Bake, uncovered, in hot oven 20 minutes; reduce heat to moderate, bake, uncovered, 1¼ hours.

Slit skin around centre of apples, trim bases so apples sit flat. Core apples, fill with prunes and rosemary; place apples on wire rack around pork, brush with pan juices. Bake in moderate oven about 1 hour or until pork and apples are tender. Cover pork loosely with foil; stand 15 minutes before slicing. Serve pork with baked apples and Caramelised Onion Jam.

Caramelised Onion Jam Heat butter in large pan, add onion, cook, stirring, about 20 minutes or until onion is very soft and browned lightly. Add sugar; stir over low heat until sugar dissolves. Simmer, uncovered, stirring occasionally, until mixture is thick and caramelised. Add vinegar; simmer, uncovered, stirring occasionally, about 5 minutes, or until mixture is thickened slightly. Stir in rosemary.

Should there be any leftovers of either the roast pork with apples or the caramelised onion jam, they are delicious served cold.

Ham

TRADITIONAL GLAZED HAM

For maximum impact and minimum fuss, nothing compares with a glazed and decorated ham in the centre of your Christmas table. Ham can be served either warm or cold, so it is easy to make it the day before it is required.

8kg cooked leg of ham
Thinly sliced glace ginger and whole cloves, to decorate
½ cup (125ml) honey

LIME GLAZE
1 cup (250ml) lime marmalade
2 tablespoons lime juice
¼ cup (50g) firmly packed brown sugar
¼ cup (60ml) sweet sherry or orange juice

Lime Glaze Combine all ingredients in small pan; stir over low heat until marmalade melts.

BARBECUE METHOD Place ham on a roasting rack or basket, or in a disposable baking dish. Cook in covered barbecue, using indirect heat, and following the manufacturer's instructions, for 1 hour. Brush ham with half the glaze; cook another 30 minutes. Decorate as desired. Brush with remaining glaze; cook about 30 minutes or until ham is well browned.

HOW TO GLAZE A HAM

Cut through rind about 10cm from shank end of leg in a decorative pattern. To remove rind, run thumb around edge of rind just under skin. Start pulling rind from widest edge of ham, continue to pull the rind carefully away from fat up to the decorative pattern. Remove rind completely. (Reserved rind can be used to cover cut surface of ham to keep it moist during storage.)

Gently cut a pattern into the ham fat. Decorate with glace ginger and cloves, or as desired. Place ham on a wire rack in a large baking dish; cover shank with foil. Brush surface of the ham with the honey; bake, uncovered, in moderate oven for 20 minutes. Remove ham from oven.

Brush ham well with Lime Glaze. Bake further 45 minutes or until browned all over, brushing frequently with glaze during cooking.

Traditional glazed ham decorated with thin slices of glace ginger, secured to the ham with whole cloves. Thin slices of orange or lime could be substituted for the ginger.

Glazes

All the glazes here are suitable to microwave. Choose large containers and low heat settings so that the glazes do not boil over.

APRICOT MUSTARD GLAZE

Apricot nectar is available bottled from supermarkets.

1 cup (250ml) apricot nectar
¼ cup (50g) firmly packed brown sugar
1 tablespoon Dijon mustard
¼ cup (60ml) orange juice
½ cup (125ml) apricot jam

Combine all ingredients in small pan; stir, over low heat, without boiling, until jam is melted, strain.

CRANBERRY-CURRANT GLAZE

340g jar redcurrant jelly
290g jar cranberry sauce
2 tablespoons lemon juice
⅓ cup (80ml) brandy

Combine jelly and sauce in medium pan; stir, over low heat, without boiling, until jelly is melted. Remove from heat; stir in juice and brandy, strain.

PINEAPPLE-ORANGE GLAZE

¼ cup (60ml) pineapple juice
2 teaspoons soy sauce
2 tablespoons orange marmalade
1 tablespoon honey
¼ cup (50g) firmly packed brown sugar
1 tablespoon brandy

Combine all ingredients in small pan; stir, over low heat, until mixture boils. Reduce heat; simmer, uncovered 10 minutes.

RUM AND GINGER GLAZE

We used an underproof rum for this recipe.

⅓ cup (75g) glace ginger
¼ cup (50g) firmly packed brown sugar
¼ cup (60ml) dark rum
1 teaspoon grated orange rind
¼ teaspoon mustard powder

Blend or process all ingredients until smooth.

APRICOT-MANGO GLAZE

*Any fruit chutney would be suitable
for making this glaze.*

½ cup (125ml) apricot jam
**¼ cup (60ml) pawpaw and
    mango chutney**
2 tablespoons brandy
⅓ cup (80ml) water
2 teaspoons Worcestershire sauce

Combine all ingredients in small pan; stir, over
low heat, without boiling until ingredients are
combined; strain.

PORT AND APPLE GLAZE

2 medium (180g) limes
1 small (150g) red capsicum
**⅓ cup (80ml) apple and
    blackcurrant juice**
2 teaspoons lime juice
2 tablespoons port
1 teaspoon soy sauce
3 teaspoons sweet chilli sauce
¼ cup (60ml) hoisin sauce
1 teaspoon Dijon mustard
1 tablespoon brown sugar

Using a vegetable peeler, peel rind thinly from
limes; cut rind into thin strips. Remove and discard seeds and membrane from capsicum; cut
capsicum into thin strips.

Combine rind and capsicum with remaining
ingredients in small pan; simmer, covered,
about 4 minutes or until strips are soft. Strain;
reserve strips and glaze separately.

CITRUS LIQUEUR GLAZE

*Cointreau and Grand Marnier are
both orange-flavoured liqueurs.*

1 medium (180g) orange
**1 cup (250ml) concentrated
    orange juice**
¼ cup (60ml) honey
**¼ cup (50g) firmly packed
    brown sugar**
½ teaspoon soy sauce
1 teaspoon French mustard
**2 tablespoons Cointreau or
    Grand Marnier**

Using a vegetable peeler, peel rind thinly from
orange. Cut rind into thin strips, drop into pan
of boiling water, boil 3 minutes; drain.

Combine undiluted juice, honey, sugar,
sauce, mustard and rind in small pan; cook,
stirring, without boiling, until sugar dissolves.
Remove from heat; stir in liqueur.

HOW TO CARVE A HAM

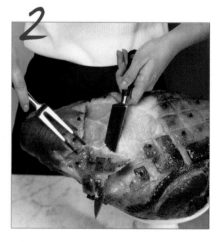

Cut a 1.5cm-deep cut in ham against the rind at
shank end. Placing knife about 7cm from cut,
slice through ham on a slight angle to meet cut;
remove wedge of ham.

Take long sweeps with the knife against the cut
surface to get long slices. The slices will increase
in size as you carve. Carve ham from sides as
well as top.

Lamb

GLAZED CORNED LEG OF LAMB

Corned (also known as "pumped") leg of lamb can be served hot or cold. You can choose one of the ham glazes for this recipe, but you will need only half the quantity. We used the citrus liqueur glaze.

1.8kg corned leg of lamb
1 litre (4 cups) water
¼ cup (60ml) white vinegar
2 tablespoons brown sugar
1 medium (150g) onion, chopped
2 bay leaves
1 sprig fresh rosemary

Place lamb in large flameproof baking dish. Pour over combined remaining ingredients. Bring to boil, cover tightly with foil. Bake in

moderately hot oven 45 minutes. Turn lamb, bake 45 minutes; drain, cool 10 minutes.

Place lamb on wire rack over clean baking dish, brush with some of the Glaze.

Bake, uncovered, in moderately hot oven for about 1 hour, brushing occasionally with

remaining Glaze or until lamb is browned. As with all corned meats, the flesh after cooking will still be a deep pink.

Glazed corned leg of lamb, above, is an unusual but delicious alternative to ham.

Vegetables

ROASTED SWEET ONIONS AND POTATOES

SERVES 8

A good accompaniment with any roast, these onions and potatoes are cooked along with a slow-cooked turkey. If using a regular roasting method, allow 1½ hours of cooking time. Halved desiree or pontiac potatoes can be substituted for kipfler potatoes.

60g butter
2 medium (280g) lemons, sliced thickly
¼ cup (55g) raw sugar
800g spring onions, trimmed
2kg kipfler potatoes
¼ cup (60ml) olive oil
12 cloves unpeeled garlic

Melt butter in baking dish, add lemon, sugar and onion; cook, stirring, until onion is slightly softened. Add whole potatoes to pan of boiling water, boil 5 minutes; drain. Dry potatoes with absorbent paper.

Below from top, roasted sweet onions and potatoes; parsley roast potatoes.

Transfer potatoes to baking dish with onion mixture; add oil and garlic. Bake, uncovered, in slow oven 2 hours. Increase temperature to moderate as for the turkey recipe; bake another 30 minutes. When turkey is removed from oven, increase temperature to hot; bake another 20 minutes or until potatoes are well browned. Turn potatoes occasionally during cooking.

PARSLEY ROAST POTATOES

SERVES 8

We found russet burbank or Idaho potatoes gave the best results. Recipe best made just before serving.

8 large (2.4kg) potatoes
16 fresh flat-leaf parsley leaves
8 cloves unpeeled garlic
½ cup (125ml) olive oil

Peel potatoes, pat dry. Cut potatoes in half crossways; trim rounded tops of potatoes to make all potatoes the same height and to sit flat. Cut a wafer-thin slice from the larger cut side of each potato, press parsley leaf onto each cut side, top with the potato slices. Place the potatoes in a greased baking dish, parsley side up, add garlic to dish; drizzle potatoes and garlic with oil. Cover potatoes with a sheet of baking paper, top with another baking dish large enough to sit on

all the potatoes; be careful not to disturb the parsley and top slices. If the top dish is not heavy enough, weight with beans or uncooked rice. Bake in moderate oven about 1 hour or until potatoes are tender. Remove top dish, baking paper and garlic. Turn oven to highest temperature; bake (or grill) potatoes until browned all over and crisp.

ASPARAGUS AND BEANS WITH CITRUS BUTTER

SERVES 8

Citrus butter can be made a week ahead. Recipe best made close to serving.

125g butter, chopped
2 teaspoons grated lemon rind
2 teaspoons grated orange rind
1 teaspoon lime rind
2 teaspoons lime juice
1½ tablespoons horseradish cream
2 bunches (500g) asparagus
500g green beans

Beat half the butter in small bowl with electric mixer until softened; beat in rinds, juice and horseradish cream. Roll butter into 15cm log on plastic wrap. Cover, refrigerate until firm.

Trim ends from asparagus and beans; cut asparagus in half. Boil, steam or microwave vegetables, separately, until just tender; drain. Toss remaining butter through hot vegetables, serve topped with sliced citrus butter.

LITTLE VEGETABLES WITH BACON ROLLS

SERVES 10

10 small (900g) red-skinned potatoes
5 small (950g) golden nugget pumpkins, quartered
20 baby carrots, trimmed
20 medium (800g) spring onions, trimmed
10 cloves unpeeled garlic
¼ cup (60ml) olive oil
1 teaspoon fine sea salt
2 teaspoons chopped fresh rosemary
7 bacon rashers

Peel potatoes in a spiral pattern, removing only half the skin. Boil for 10 minutes; drain. Combine potatoes, pumpkin, carrots, onions, garlic, oil, salt and rosemary in large baking dish; mix well. Bake, uncovered, in moderate oven 50 minutes, stirring occasionally. Remove pumpkin, carrots and onions from dish. Cut

each bacon rasher into 3 strips lengthways; roll up and secure with toothpicks. Add bacon rolls to potato mixture in dish; bake, uncovered, in moderately hot oven about 15 minutes or until bacon is crisp. Remove toothpicks from bacon. Return vegetables to the dish; bake, uncovered, 5 minutes or until hot.

HONEY MUSTARD VEGETABLES

SERVES 8

Kumara is an orange-fleshed sweet potato.
Recipe best made close to serving.

3 large (600g) onions, quartered
6 medium (720g) carrots, chopped
2 medium (800g) kumara, sliced
1/3 cup (80ml) olive oil
60g butter, melted
1/3 cup (80ml) honey
1 tablespoon seeded mustard
1 tablespoon sesame seeds, toasted

Combine vegetables in large baking dish; drizzle with half the oil. Bake, uncovered, in moderate oven about 1 hour or until vegetables are just tender. Combine butter with remaining oil, honey and mustard; pour over vegetables in dish. Bake further 20 minutes or until vegetables are soft and glaze is thickened slightly. Sprinkle with sesame seeds.

✦ It is best to cook green vegetables as close to serving as possible, but you can hasten the final cooking time by first blanching them in boiling water, then refreshing them in cold water. Drain them well and keep, covered, in the refrigerator until required. When you are ready to serve the vegetables, drop them into a large pan of boiling water and return quickly to the boil; drain and serve as desired.

✦ For perfect crunchy potatoes every time, peel large potatoes and cut into desired size — wedges are particularly good cooked this way. Place the potatoes in a large pan; add enough water to just cover them. Bring potatoes to the boil; drain. Place potatoes on lightly greased oven trays; brush lightly with oil. Bake, uncovered, in hot oven about 30 minutes (time will vary depending on size of pieces) or until crisp outside and cooked through.

When all else is en fête, *why not dress up the vegetables as well? From top, asparagus and beans with citrus butter; little vegetables with bacon rolls; honey mustard vegetables.*

Seafood

SEAFOOD PLATTER

SERVES 8 TO 10 AS AN ENTREE

SERVES 4 TO 6 AS A MAIN COURSE

This is a marinated mix cooked on the barbecue or in a griddle pan. Octopus and calamari can be marinated up to 2 days ahead and kept, covered, under refrigeration. The sauces can be made a day ahead. Whether served hot or cold, this recipe is best made close to serving.

600g baby octopus
2 large (500g) squid hoods
1/3 cup (80ml) olive oil
1/3 cup (80ml) lemon juice
3 cloves garlic, crushed
2 teaspoons chopped fresh thyme
12 (500g) cooked king prawns
600g white fish fillets
1/3 cup (50g) plain flour
1 tablespoon Cajun seasoning
Thai-style sweet chilli sauce

SALSA-TOPPED OYSTERS

12 fresh oysters
1/2 small (100g) red onion, chopped finely
1/2 small (60g) egg tomato, seeded, chopped finely
1 tablespoon lime juice
1 tablespoon balsamic vinegar
1 tablespoon olive oil

TARTARE SAUCE

1 cup mayonnaise
2 large gherkins, chopped finely
2 tablespoons drained capers, chopped
1 tablespoon chopped fresh parsley
1 teaspoon lemon juice
1/2 teaspoon Worcestershire sauce

COCKTAIL SAUCE

1 cup mayonnaise
1/3 cup (80ml) tomato sauce
1/2 teaspoon Worcestershire sauce
1/2 teaspoon chilli sauce

Remove and discard heads and beaks from octopus, cut octopus in half. Cut squid hoods open, cut shallow diagonal slashes in criss-cross pattern on inside surface; cut each hood into 4 pieces. Combine octopus and squid in bowl with oil, juice, garlic and thyme. Cover; refrigerate several hours or overnight, stirring occasionally.

Shell and devein prawns, leaving heads and tails intact. Cut fish fillets into thick strips, toss in combined flour and Cajun seasoning. Heat barbecue or griddle pan; add fish, drained octopus and squid in batches, cook until just tender.

Serve hot or cold fish, octopus, squid and prawns with chilli sauce, Salsa-topped Oysters, Tartare Sauce and Cocktail Sauce.

Salsa-topped Oysters Remove oysters from shells; wash and dry shells. Return oysters to shells, top with combined remaining ingredients.

Tartare Sauce Combine all ingredients in medium bowl; mix well.

Cocktail Sauce Combine all ingredients in medium bowl; mix well.

Fresh Seafood with Two Sauces

SERVES 8 TO 10 AS AN ENTREE
SERVES 4 TO 6 AS A MAIN COURSE

*These sauces are great with most seafood;
choose the type of seafood you prefer. Both of
them can be made a day ahead and kept,
covered, under refrigeration. Nam pla is an
Asian fish sauce and wasabi is prepared
Japanese horseradish; both are available
from Asian specialty stores.*

1 cooked lobster
2 cooked blue-swimmer crabs
12 (500g) cooked king prawns
375g sliced smoked salmon
Lemon and lime wedges

GINGER AND LEMON GRASS SAUCE
¹/₂ cup (125ml) white vinegar
¹/₂ cup (110g) sugar
¹/₄ cup (60ml) water
1 stalk fresh lemon grass, sliced finely
2cm piece fresh ginger, shredded
2 tablespoons nam pla

HORSERADISH AND DILL CREAM
300g carton sour cream
2 tablespoons horseradish cream
2 tablespoons chopped fresh dill
1 teaspoon wasabi
2 teaspoons lemon juice

Clean and prepare all seafood, leaving shells
intact if desired. Serve with lemon and lime
wedges and Ginger and Lemon Grass Sauce and
Horseradish and Dill Cream.

Ginger and Lemon Grass Sauce Combine vinegar, sugar, water, lemon grass and ginger in small pan; cook, stirring, without boiling, until sugar dissolves. Bring to boil then simmer 7 minutes or until sauce thickens slightly. Stir in nam pla; cool.

Horseradish and Dill Cream Combine all ingredients in small bowl; mix well.

*Sauces add zest to both the barbecued seafood
platter, opposite, and the cold platter of fresh
seafood, above.*

Desserts

Puddings

CHRISTMAS PUDDING WITH HOMEMADE CITRUS PEEL

SERVES 10 TO 12

It is well worth the extra effort to make your own citrus peel for this traditional pudding recipe. Cooked in a cloth and either boiled or steamed, puddings can be made 2 months ahead and kept in the refrigerator in a freezer bag or airtight container. Puddings (or leftovers) can be frozen for 12 months and reheated in the microwave oven. Bicarbonate of soda is also known as baking soda.

**1½ cups (250g) chopped
    seeded dates**
1²/3 cups (250g) dried currants
³/4 cup (120g) sultanas
³/4 cup (120g) chopped raisins
**1/3 cup (80ml) Cointreau or
    orange juice**
½ teaspoon bicarbonate of soda
1 tablespoon boiling water
250g soft butter
**2½ cups (500g) firmly packed dark
    brown sugar**
4 eggs
1 cup (150g) plain flour
1 teaspoon ground ginger
4 cups (280g) stale breadcrumbs

CITRUS PEEL
2 large (600g) oranges
1 medium (140g) lemon
1 cup (250ml) water
2 cups (440g) sugar

CITRUS BUTTER
250g butter

Combine fruit and liqueur in large bowl. Add combined soda and water; mix well. Cover, stand overnight at room temperature.

Beat butter and sugar in medium bowl with electric mixer until just combined (do not over-beat). Add eggs, 1 at a time, beating only until combined between additions. Stir butter mixture into fruit mixture with Citrus Peel and 2 table-spoons of the reserved syrup from the peel. Stir in sifted flour and ginger, then breadcrumbs. Boil or steam, as directed on pp 26 and 27. Serve hot pudding with Citrus Butter.

Citrus Peel Peel rind thickly from oranges and lemon, including the white pith. Add rind to pan of boiling water; simmer, uncovered, 10 minutes. Drain, repeat. Combine 1 cup water and sugar in medium pan; stir over heat, without boiling, until sugar dissolves. Add rind, simmer, uncovered, 10 minutes. Remove from heat; stand 10 minutes, transfer to heatproof bowl, stand rind in syrup overnight. Return rind and syrup to clean pan; simmer, uncovered, 20 minutes. Remove rind from syrup; cool rind, reserve syrup (you need about 1¼ cups/310ml syrup). Chop rind into pieces about the size of a currant.

Citrus Butter Beat butter in small bowl with electric mixer until as white as possible. Gradually beat in 1 cup (250ml) of the cooled reserved syrup. Transfer mixture to piping bag fitted with star tube, pipe rosettes onto baking paper-covered tray. Cover, refrigerate or freeze until firm.

This handsome boiled pudding with homemade citrus peel is one variation using the above ingredients. The mixture can also be steamed or divided into smaller portions for mini puds for a lovely gift idea.

BOILED PUDDING

SERVES 10 TO 12

*You need a 60cm square of unbleached calico.
If the fabric is new, soak in cold water
overnight, then boil for 20 minutes;
rinse well before using.*

Have ready a large boiler three-quarters full of
rapidly boiling water, 2.5m of kitchen string and
$1/2$ cup (75g) plain flour.

Wearing thick rubber gloves, dip prepared
pudding cloth into boiling water; boil 1 minute.
Squeeze excess water from cloth.

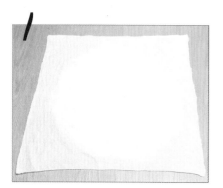

Working quickly, spread hot cloth on bench. Rub
flour into centre of cloth to cover an area about
40cm in diameter, leaving flour thicker in the
centre where the "skin" will need to be thickest.

Place cloth into medium bowl then place
pudding mixture in centre; gather cloth evenly
around pudding. Lift pudding out of bowl, pat
into a round shape. Tie cloth tightly with string
as close to mixture as possible. Tie a loop in
string to make pudding easy to handle. Pull ends
tightly to make pudding as round as possible.

Gently lower pudding into boiling water;
cover with tight-fitting lid, boil rapidly for
6 hours. Replenish with boiling water as required.

Place handle of wooden spoon through loop
of string, lift from water. Suspend pudding from
spoon by placing over rungs of an up-turned
stool or wedging a handle in a drawer; pudding
should swing freely. Twist wet ends of cloth
around supporting string away from pudding.
Hang pudding 10 minutes or until cloth is dry
around pudding. Place pudding in a medium
bowl, cut string, carefully peel back cloth a
little. Invert pudding onto a plate, carefully
pull back cloth completely; cool. Wrap pudding
in plastic wrap, seal tightly in freezer bag or airtight container; refrigerate or freeze.

MINI BOILED PUDDINGS

MAKES 4

Cut 4 x 40cm squares of unbleached calico.
Prepare one cloth at a time as for large pudding.
Use $1/4$ cup (35g) plain flour for each cloth. Divide
mixture evenly between cloths. Tie puddings as
for large pudding. Boil rapidly for 4 hours.

STEAMED PUDDING

SERVES 10 TO 12

Grease pudding steamer (2.25 litre/9-cup
capacity). Spoon pudding mixture into prepared
steamer. Top with pleated baking paper and
foil, secure with string or lid. Place pudding in
large boiler with enough boiling water to come
halfway up side of steamer. Cover boiler with
tight-fitting lid; boil 6 hours. Replenish with
boiling water as required. Stand pudding
15 minutes before turning onto a plate; cool.

Wrap pudding in plastic wrap, return to clean steamer, or seal tightly in freezer bag or airtight container; refrigerate or freeze.

TO REHEAT PUDDINGS

Thaw frozen puddings 2 days in refrigerator. Remove pudding from refrigerator 12 hours before reheating.

Boiled Remove plastic wrap and tie clean dry unfloured cloth on pudding. Boil 2 hours following cooking instructions; allow 1 hour for mini puddings. Hang hot puddings 10 minutes; remove from cloth. Stand pudding 20 minutes for skin to darken.

Steamed Remove plastic wrap and return pudding to steamer. Steam 2 hours following cooking instructions.

Microwave Reheat 4 single serves at once. Cover with microwave-safe plastic wrap; microwave on HIGH (100%) up to 1 minute per serve. To reheat whole pudding, cover with microwave-safe plastic wrap, microwave on MEDIUM (50%) about 15 minutes or until hot.

Equally delicious and attractive, the steamed version of the pudding with homemade citrus peel, above. *Sliced oranges are a simple yet stylish alternative decoration to the traditional holly.* At left, *a mini-boiled pudding sits gift-wrapped for Christmas.*

MICROWAVE CHRISTMAS PUDDING

SERVES 6

This pudding can be made ahead. Store, covered, in the refrigerator for a week, or in the freezer for 2 months.

125g butter
¾ cup (150g) firmly packed brown sugar
2 eggs
2 teaspoons golden syrup

1 tablespoon Parisian essence
1¼ cups (250g) dried mixed fruit
½ cup (110g) canned pie apples
¾ cup (110g) plain flour
½ teaspoon ground cinnamon
¼ teaspoon ground nutmeg
¼ teaspoon ground ginger
1 cup (70g) stale breadcrumbs
¼ cup (60ml) sweet sherry

Grease a 1.5litre/6-cup capacity microwave-safe bowl. Beat butter and sugar in small bowl with electric mixer until light and fluffy. Add eggs, 1 at a time, beating well between additions; beat in golden syrup and essence. Stir in fruit, pie apples, sifted flour and spices, breadcrumbs and sherry. Spoon mixture into prepared bowl. Cook, uncovered, on LOW (30%) for about 35 minutes or until cooked when tested. Stand for 15 minutes before serving.

Here's a wonderful marriage of modern microwave technology and an old-fashioned process. The Christmas microwave pudding, below, tastes as good as it looks, but takes only 35 minutes to cook.

CHRISTMAS FRUIT BOMBE

SERVES 8

*Bombe can be made a week ahead;
cover tightly with plastic wrap.*

2 litres vanilla ice-cream
¹/₃ cup (75g) chopped
**   glace pineapple**
¹/₃ cup (85g) chopped glace apricots
¹/₃ cup (70g) halved red
**   glace cherries**
¹/₄ cup (50g) chopped glace ginger
1 teaspoon mixed spice
1 teaspoon ground cinnamon
700g round (approximately 18cm)
**   rich fruit cake**

BRANDY CREAM SAUCE
300ml thickened cream
¹/₄ cup brandy
2 eggs, separated
¹/₂ cup (110g) caster sugar

Lightly grease a pudding steamer (1.75ml/
7-cup capacity), line with plastic wrap.

Combine softened ice-cream and fruit in
large bowl, stir in spices. Spoon mixture into
prepared basin, cover tightly with plastic wrap;
freeze for about 1 hour or until just firm. Split
cake in half, trim one half to fit top of ice-cream
(remaining half is not used in this recipe),
press on gently; cover and freeze until firm.

To serve, invert bombe onto a serving plate;
remove all plastic wrap. Serve with Brandy
Cream Sauce.

Brandy Cream Sauce Beat cream and brandy in
medium bowl with electric mixer until soft
peaks form. Beat egg whites in small bowl with
electric mixer until soft peaks form; gradually
add sugar, beating until sugar dissolves. Beat
in egg yolks. Fold egg white mixture into
cream mixture.

*Above, a cool change for a hot Yuletide, this
Christmas fruit bombe includes glace fruits and
mixed spices, just like the steamed classic.*

Sauces

ORANGE HARD SAUCE

MAKES ABOUT 2 CUPS

Grand Marnier is an orange-flavoured liqueur. Refrigerate sauce for up to a week or freeze for 2 months.

250g soft butter
2 tablespoons finely grated
orange rind

½ cup (80g) icing sugar mixture
¼ cup (60ml) cream
⅓ cup (80ml) Grand Marnier

Beat butter, rind and icing sugar in small bowl with electric mixer until as white as possible; beat in cream and liqueur. Spoon mixture into serving bowl. If you prefer, mixture can be shaped into logs: divide mixture in half; roll each half into 2cm-diameter log shape; then wrap in foil or greaseproof paper, twisting ends to secure. Refrigerate logs for about 2 hours or until firm.

CREAMY CARAMEL SAUCE

MAKES ABOUT 2 CUPS

Kahlua is a coffee-flavoured liqueur. Sauce can be made a day ahead; keep, covered, in refrigerator. Reheat gently just before serving.

¾ cup (165g) caster sugar
½ cup (125ml) water
¾ cup (180ml) cream
60g butter
2 tablespoons Kahlua

FLUFFY WHITE SAUCE

MAKES ABOUT 3 CUPS

This is a sauce best prepared close to serving time.

30g butter
1 tablespoon plain flour
1/3 cup (75g) caster sugar
1/2 cup (125ml) milk
2 teaspoons vanilla essence
2 egg whites
3/4 cup (180ml) cream

Heat butter in small pan, add flour and sugar; cook, stirring, until combined. Gradually stir in milk; cook, stirring, until mixture boils and thickens; stir in vanilla essence. Transfer sauce to large bowl; cover the surface tightly with plastic wrap; cool.

Beat egg whites in small bowl with electric mixer until soft peaks form, fold into sauce. Beat cream in small bowl until soft peaks form; fold into sauce. Serve immediately.

CINNAMON BRANDY CUSTARD

MAKES ABOUT 3 CUPS

This custard can be made 2 days ahead and kept, covered, under refrigeration. Reheat, uncovered, without boiling, just before serving.

6 egg yolks
1/3 cup (75g) caster sugar
2 cups (500ml) milk
300ml cream
1 cinnamon stick
1 1/2 tablespoons brandy

Beat egg yolks and sugar in medium bowl with electric mixer until thick and creamy. Combine milk, cream and cinnamon stick in large pan; bring to boil. Remove from heat; remove and reserve cinnamon stick. Gradually whisk milk mixture into egg mixture. Return mixture and cinnamon stick to pan, stir over low heat, without boiling, until custard thickens and coats the back of a metal spoon. Discard cinnamon stick; stir in brandy.

Combine sugar and water in medium pan; stir over heat, without boiling, until sugar dissolves. Boil, without stirring, until dark golden. Carefully add cream to toffee in pan (the cream will bubble quite fiercely and mixture will harden). Boil, stirring, until toffee dissolves. Remove from heat; stir in butter and liqueur. Serve warm.

Above from left to right, *orange hard sauce, creamy caramel sauce, fluffy white sauce* and, right, *cinnamon brandy custard — four delicious alternatives to dress up your pudding.*

Cakes & other sweet treats

RICH HAZELNUT FRUIT CAKE

Richly flavoured with hazelnuts, this cake can be made up to six months ahead. Store in a cool dry place or refrigerate if the weather is humid. Frangelico is a hazelnut-flavoured liqueur; substitute brandy, if desired. Nutella is a chocolate hazelnut spread.

2¹/₃ cups (375g) sultanas
2¹/₄ cups (375g) chopped raisins
1¹/₂ cups (250g) chopped
  seeded dates
1¹/₄ cups (240g) chopped
  seeded prunes
2 tablespoons raspberry jam,
  warmed, sieved
²/₃ cup (160g) Frangelico
185g butter, chopped
¹/₃ cup (85g) Nutella
1 cup (200g) firmly packed
  brown sugar
4 eggs
1³/₄ cups (260g) plain flour
¹/₄ cup (25g) cocoa powder
1 teaspoon ground nutmeg
1 teaspoon ground cinnamon
1 cup (150g) roasted
  hazelnuts, chopped
¹/₄ cup (60ml) Frangelico, extra

Combine fruit, jam and liqueur in large bowl, cover; stand at room temperature overnight or up to 1 week.

Line base and side of deep 22cm round or deep 19cm square cake pan with 1 layer brown paper and 3 layers baking paper, bringing paper 5cm above edge of pan.

Beat butter, Nutella and sugar in small bowl with electric mixer until just combined (do not overbeat). Add eggs, 1 at a time, beating until just combined between additions. Stir butter mixture into fruit mixture along with the sifted dry ingredients and nuts.

Spread mixture into prepared pan. Bake in slow oven about 3¹/₂ hours. Brush hot cake with extra liqueur. Cover hot cake with foil; allow to cool in pan.

LITTLE GIFT CAKES

MAKES 18

For the bold icing colours essential to these little gift cakes, we used powdered food colourings, available from cake decoration suppliers and some health food stores. We found that mixing the powder with a very small amount of hot water before being kneaded into fondant gives a better result. Liquid colourings can be used for paler colours. To give as gifts, the cakes can be placed on pieces of thick cardboard, measuring about 9cm square, covered with special foil or glossy gift paper. Gift cakes can be made a month ahead; store in an airtight container at room temperature.

1 square Melt 'n' Mix Fruit Cake
2 x 500g packets soft icing (fondant)
³/₄ cup (180ml) apricot jam,
  warmed, sieved
Icing sugar mixture
Food colourings
Ribbons and decorations

Cut cake into 9 even pieces, split each in half horizontally; cover to keep airtight.

Knead fondant until smooth on surface dusted with icing sugar. Divide fondant into as many pieces as there are different colours to be used. Tint each piece by kneading in one of the prepared colourings — leave some pieces uncoloured if white icing is desired. Wrap tinted pieces individually in plastic wrap until ready to use.

Brush top and sides of each cake evenly with jam just before it is ready to be covered with fondant. Divide fondant so that you have 18 pieces in total; roll out each piece between sheets of baking paper until large enough to cover top and sides of each cake. Lift fondant onto cake, then lightly mould fondant over cake with sugared hands; trim edges neatly. Repeat with remaining fondant and cakes. Scraps can be cut to make decorative shapes — we used moons, stars and spots. Secure shapes to cakes with a little more jam. Decorate cakes with ribbons and decorations.

MELT 'N' MIX FRUIT CAKE

This cake can be made 2 months ahead and stored in an airtight container or refrigerated if weather is humid. We used the square version of this cake for the little gift cakes, but it can also be cooked in a deep 22cm round cake pan. Bicarbonate of soda is also known as baking soda.

5 cups (1kg) mixed dried fruit
¹/₄ cup (35g) slivered
  almonds, toasted
2 tablespoons sweet sherry
1¹/₄ cups (250g) firmly packed
  brown sugar
250g butter, chopped
¹/₂ cup (125ml) milk
3 eggs, beaten lightly
3 cups (450g) plain flour
¹/₂ teaspoon bicarbonate of soda
2 teaspoons mixed spice

Grease deep 19cm square cake pan, cover base and sides with 3 layers of baking paper, bringing paper 5cm above edge of pan.

Combine fruit, nuts, sherry and sugar in large bowl. Combine butter and milk in small pan; stir over heat, without boiling, until butter melts. Add butter mixture, eggs and sifted dry ingredients to fruit mixture; mix well. Spread mixture into prepared pan. Bake in very slow oven about 5 hours. Cover hot cake with foil. Turn cake onto board; cool upside down in pan.

Opposite, a rich hazelnut fruit cake sits proud among a flurry of little gift cakes made from the Melt 'n' Mix Fruit Cake recipe. Iced in bold colours, these individual cakes are a super gift idea for office colleagues, the children's teachers or relatives 'who have everything'.

PINEAPPLE AND CARROT FRUIT CAKE

You need about 2 large carrots for this recipe. The cake can be made 2 weeks ahead and stored in an airtight container in the refrigerator.

1³/4 cups (280g) chopped
    seeded dates
1¹/2 cups (250g) sultanas
450g can crushed pineapple
    in heavy syrup
1¹/2 cups (360g) coarsely
    grated carrot
¹/2 cup (60g) chopped walnuts
125g butter, chopped
1 cup (200g) firmly packed
    brown sugar
¹/2 teaspoon bicarbonate of soda
2 eggs, beaten lightly
1 cup (150g) plain flour
1 cup (150g) self-raising flour
1 teaspoon ground cinnamon

Line deep 20cm round cake pan with 3 layers of baking paper, bringing paper 5cm above edge of pan. Combine dates, sultanas, undrained pineapple, carrot, nuts, butter and sugar in large pan; stir over heat, without boiling, until sugar dissolves. Simmer, uncovered, about 10 minutes or until mixture is thick and syrupy.

Remove from heat, stir in soda. Transfer mixture to large bowl; cool to room temperature. Stir eggs and sifted dry ingredients into fruit mixture, spread into prepared pan. Bake in slow oven about 2¹/2 hours. Cover hot cake with foil; cool in pan.

GOLDEN CHERRY AND ALMOND CAKE

Almond-flavoured Amaretto liqueur combines beautifully with the cherries. This cake can be made up to a month ahead and stored in the refrigerator.

185g butter, chopped
1 cup (220g) caster sugar
3 eggs
1 cup (200g) fruit mince
²/3 cup (110g) blanched
    almonds, halved
¹/3 cup (85g) quartered red
    glace cherries
¹/3 cup (85g) quartered green
    glace cherries
1 cup (150g) plain flour
¹/2 cup (75g) self-raising flour
¹/4 cup (60ml) Amaretto liqueur

Line base and side of deep 20cm round cake pan with 1 layer brown paper and 3 layers baking paper; bringing paper 5cm above edge of pan.

Beat butter and sugar in small bowl with electric mixer until combined; beat in eggs, 1 at a time, until combined. Transfer mixture to large bowl, stir in remaining ingredients. Spread mixture into prepared pan. Bake in moderately slow oven about 1¹/2 hours. Cover cake with foil; cool in pan.

Pineapple and carrot fruit cake, opposite, and golden cherry and almond cake, below, are two light alternatives to traditional Christmas cakes.

FESTIVE FRUIT AND NUT CAKE

This cake can be made 3 months ahead and kept refrigerated in an airtight container.

3 rings (85g) glace pineapple, chopped coarsely
½ cup (125g) coarsely chopped glace apricots
1½ cups (250g) seeded dates
½ cup (105g) red glace cherries
½ cup (105g) green glace cherries
¾ cup (120g) blanched almonds
1½ cups (250g) Brazil nuts
2 eggs
½ cup (100g) firmly packed brown sugar
1 tablespoon dark underproof rum
90g soft butter
⅓ cup (50g) plain flour
¼ cup (35g) self-raising flour
1½ teaspoons gelatine
1 tablespoon water

FRUIT TOPPING

4 rings (125g) glace pineapple, roughly chopped
¼ cup (50g) red glace cherries, halved
¼ cup (50g) green glace cherries, halved
⅔ cup (110g) Brazil nuts
⅔ cup (110g) blanched almonds

Grease two 8cm x 26cm bar cake pans, line base with baking paper, bringing paper 5cm above opposite long sides.

Combine pineapple, apricots and remaining whole fruit and nuts in large bowl. Beat eggs in small bowl with electric mixer until thick and creamy; add sugar, rum and butter, beat until just combined. Stir egg mixture into fruit mixture with sifted flours. Press cake mixture firmly into prepared pans.

Arrange Fruit Topping over cake mixture. Bake, uncovered, in slow oven for 1 hour; cover cakes with foil, bake 45 minutes. Stand cakes in pans 10 minutes, turn cakes carefully onto wire racks to cool. Sprinkle gelatine over water in cup; stand cup in small pan of simmering water, stirring until gelatine dissolves; cool slightly. Brush gelatine mixture over Fruit Topping.

Fruit Topping Combine all ingredients in medium bowl; mix well.

TOFFEE NUT RING

A variation on the festive fruit and nut cake substituting spun toffee and nuts for the fruit topping. Nut topping and spun toffee can be made 2 hours ahead if weather is not humid. Keep cake in an airtight container at all times.

1 quantity Festive Fruit and Nut Cake mixture

NUT TOPPING

1½ cups (330g) caster sugar
1½ cups (375ml) water
½ cup (50g) pecans, toasted
⅔ cup (110g) Brazil nuts, toasted
⅓ cup (55g) blanched almonds, toasted
⅓ cup (50g) macadamias, toasted

SPUN TOFFEE

¾ cup (165g) sugar
¾ cup (180ml) water

Grease deep 20cm ring pan, line base with baking paper. Press cake mixture firmly into prepared pan. Bake in slow oven about 2 hours; cover with foil if overbrowning. Stand cake in pan 10 minutes; turn onto wire rack to cool.

Nut Topping Have a baking dish one-third full with simmering water. Meanwhile combine sugar and the measured water in medium pan; stir over heat, without boiling, until sugar dissolves. Bring to boil; boil, uncovered, without stirring, until a rich caramel colour. Pour one-third of the toffee over half the cake; stand pan in baking dish to keep toffee liquid. Quickly arrange half the nuts on toffee on cake. Repeat on other side of cake with half the remaining toffee and the remaining nuts; drizzle all over with the remaining toffee. You may need to reheat toffee gently if it sets too quickly. Gather up Spun Toffee, place over nuts close to serving; keep airtight.

Spun Toffee Lightly oil 2 oven trays. Combine sugar and water in medium pan, stir over heat, without boiling, until sugar dissolves. Bring to boil; boil, uncovered, without stirring, until a rich caramel colour. Using a fork, drizzle toffee in thin strands over prepared trays. Use immediately.

The spectacular toffee nut ring, right, is based on the festive fruit and nut cake, far right, and both are proven favourites at many Christmas gatherings.

Mince pies

SPICED FRUIT MINCE

MAKES 14 CUPS

Dark underproof rum, sherry or orange juice can substitute for the brandy in this traditional mince. Mixture should be made at least 3 days before using.

4¹/₂ cups (750g) sultanas
4¹/₂ cups (750g) raisins, chopped
3¹/₂ cups (450g) dried currants
3 cups (500g) seeded dates, chopped
3¹/₂ cups (500g) seeded prunes, chopped
2 large (400g) green-skinned apples, peeled, grated
1 cup (200g) firmly packed brown sugar
2 tablespoons finely grated orange rind
1 tablespoon mixed spice
2 teaspoons ground cloves
¹/₂ cup (125ml) plum jam
1¹/₂ cups (375ml) brandy

Mix all ingredients in large bowl. Cover tightly with plastic wrap. Store mixture in cool dark place or refrigerator for 3 days before using; stir mixture once a day. Mixture can be kept, covered, under refrigeration, up to 6 months.

FRUIT MINCE PIES

MAKES 24

You can use either the spiced fruit mince mixture above or purchased bottled fruit mince in this recipe. Mince pies can be made a week ahead and stored in an airtight container. They can also be frozen for up to a month.

2 cups (300g) plain flour
150g butter
1 teaspoon finely grated orange rind
1 tablespoon vegetable oil
2 tablespoons caster sugar
1 egg, beaten lightly
1 tablespoon water, approximately
2¹/₂ cups (500g) fruit mince
1 egg, beaten lightly, extra

Sift flour into medium bowl, rub in butter; stir in rind, oil and sugar (or process flour, butter, rind, oil and sugar until crumbly).

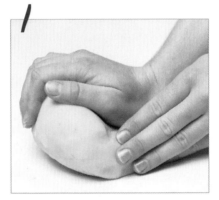

Add egg and enough water to make ingredients cling together (or process until ingredients just come together). Turn onto floured surface; knead until smooth. Cover pastry, refrigerate 30 minutes. Roll two-thirds of the pastry between sheets of baking paper until 3mm thick. Cut 24 x 7.5cm rounds from pastry, re-rolling dough as necessary to make 24 rounds.

The spiced fruit mince, opposite, is best if left to mature for several days before use in pies and tarts, above.

Place rounds into two greased 12-hole (2 table-spoons/40ml capacity) patty pan trays. Divide fruit mince among pastry cases. Roll remaining pastry between sheets of baking paper until 3mm thick. Cut 12 x 5cm rounds from remaining pastry, re-rolling dough as necessary. Using cover stencil (or use a small biscuit/cookie cutter), cut small stars from each round. Top half the pies with the rounds; top remaining pies with the star cut-outs. Brush pastry rounds and stars with extra egg.

Bake in moderate oven about 20 minutes, or until browned. Transfer to wire rack to cool. Serve dusted with sifted icing sugar, if desired.

shortbread

SCOTTISH SHORTBREAD

MAKES 16

If you use wooden moulds, do not grease them but rub cornflour firmly into the shortbread pattern in the mould. The natural oils from your fingers will make the cornflour stick to the moulds. Do not wash the mould after use; just brush any cornflour out of the mould and store in a dry place. Shortbread can be made a week ahead and stored in an airtight container.

250g butter, chopped
1/3 cup (75g) caster sugar
1/4 cup (35g) rice flour
2 1/4 cups (335g) plain flour

Beat butter and sugar in small bowl with electric mixer until smooth. Stir in sifted flours; press mixture together to form a firm dough. Knead gently on floured surface until smooth.

Scottish shortbread can be cooked in many ways:

✦ Press mixture into greased 19cm x 29cm rectangular slice pan; mark as desired, prick with fork. Bake in slow oven 45 minutes. Cut where marked while warm; stand shortbread in pan 10 minutes before turning onto wire rack to cool.

✦ Divide mixture between two 17cm round sandwich cake pans; press dough down into pan, smooth tops. Mark each round into 8 wedges, prick with fork in decorative pattern. Bake in slow oven 45 minutes. Cut where marked while warm; stand shortbread in pans 10 minutes before turning onto wire racks to cool.

✦ Cornflour an 11cm wooden shortbread mould; tap out excess cornflour. Press about an eighth of the mixture into prepared mould. Cut away excess dough, tap mould on base to release dough onto greased oven tray. Repeat with remaining dough. Bake in slow oven about 30 minutes or until firm. Stand shortbread on tray 5 minutes before lifting onto wire racks to cool.

BUTTERY SHORTBREAD WITH ALMONDS

MAKES 16

Shortbread can be made a week ahead and stored in an airtight container.

250g butter, chopped
1/4 cup (35g) rice flour
1 3/4 cups (260g) plain flour
2/3 cup (110g) icing sugar mixture
1 egg white, beaten lightly
3/4 cup (60g) flaked almonds

Grease two 20cm round sandwich cake pans. Process butter, flours and icing sugar until mixture forms a ball. Knead gently on floured surface until smooth. Press half of dough into each of the prepared pans; smooth tops. Mark each round into 8 wedges, prick with fork, brush with egg white. Overlap almonds in rows on each wedge. Bake in moderately slow oven about 45 minutes or until browned lightly. Cut where marked while warm; stand in pan to cool.

CHOCOLATE SHORTBREAD

MAKES 16

Shortbread can be made a week ahead and stored in an airtight container.

250g butter, chopped
1 cup (160g) icing sugar mixture
1 1/4 cups (185g) plain flour
1/2 cup (75g) rice flour
1/4 cup (25g) cocoa powder
2 tablespoons sugar

Grease two 20cm round sandwich cake pans. Beat butter and icing sugar mixture in small bowl with electric mixer until smooth; stir in sifted flours and cocoa. Press half of dough into each of the prepared pans; smooth tops. Mark each round into 8 wedges, prick with fork in decorative pattern; sprinkle with sugar. Bake in moderately slow oven about 45 minutes or until just firm to touch. Cut where marked while warm; stand in pan to cool.

Buttery shortbread with almonds and chocolate shortbread, opposite, are two alternatives to the traditional Scottish shortbread shown left.

Gingerbread

GINGERBREAD HOUSE

A gingerbread house can be assembled 3 days ahead; bake gingerbread a day before required and store in an airtight container. Bicarbonate of soda is also known as baking soda.

90g butter
1 cup (200g) firmly packed brown
  sugar
1 cup (250ml) honey
2 teaspoons finely grated lemon rind

2 eggs, beaten lightly
5 cups (750g) plain flour
1 cup (150g) self-raising flour
1 teaspoon bicarbonate of soda
2 teaspoons ground ginger
1½ teaspoons ground cinnamon
1 teaspoon ground cloves
½ teaspoon ground nutmeg
½ teaspoon ground cardamom
Assorted sweets

GLAZE

1 tablespoon caster sugar
2 tablespoons water
½ teaspoon powdered gelatine

ROYAL ICING

2 egg whites
4 cups (640g) pure icing sugar,
  approximately
½ teaspoon lemon juice

Combine butter, sugar and honey in medium pan; stir over low heat until sugar dissolves, cool 10 minutes. Transfer mixture to large bowl; stir in rind, eggs and sifted dry ingredients. Turn dough onto floured surface, knead gently until mixture loses its stickiness; cover; refrigerate 1 hour.

Cut paper patterns for gingerbread house: cut two rectangles, each 20cm x 15cm, for roof; two rectangles, each 15cm x 10cm, for sides; and one rectangle, 16cm wide x 19cm high, for front/back. Trim front/back rectangle so that sides are 10cm high, as shown in **Pic 1**.

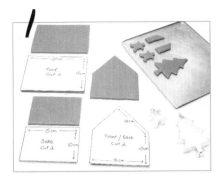

Roll out dough on floured surface until 1cm thick; cut shapes from dough using paper patterns, re-rolling dough as necessary. Cut Christmas tree and small gingerbread people using biscuit cutters, then cut two chimney shapes about 6cm high from leftover dough. Place shapes on lightly greased oven trays. Bake in moderately hot oven about 10 minutes or until firm. Stand gingerbread on trays 5 minutes, brush with glaze. Transfer glazed gingerbread to wire racks to cool. Cut door from front of house. Cover a small board or tray with foil, spread a thin layer of Royal Icing over foil to represent snow; scrape over surface slightly with a fork to roughen.

Assemble gingerbread house as shown, using Icing to secure pieces together. Using Icing, join chimney pieces to roof. Stick cotton wool on top to represent smoke, if desired. Add a little water to a small amount of Icing; use this to put peaks of snow on underside of roof. Use Icing to secure sweets to house, decorating as desired. Place tree and people on board; create a fence around house with sweets. Lightly dust house with a little extra sifted icing sugar and decorate edge of board with ribbon, if desired.

Glaze Combine all ingredients in small pan; stir over low heat, without boiling, until sugar and gelatine dissolve.

Royal Icing Beat egg whites in small bowl with electric mixer until just frothy; gradually beat in enough sifted icing sugar for mixture to form very stiff peaks, stir in juice. Keep the surface of the icing covered with a damp tea-towel to prevent it drying out.

CHRISTMAS GINGERBREAD BISCUITS

MAKES ABOUT 40

For bold decoration colours on this gingerbread, we used powdered food colourings, available from cake decorating suppliers and some health food stores. We found mixing the powder with a small amount of hot water before stirring into the icing gives a better result; liquid colourings can be used for pale colours. Gold and silver cachous are small ball-shaped sugar decorations, available from supermarkets. Decorated gingerbread shapes can be made 2 weeks ahead and stored in an airtight container.

125g soft butter
1/2 cup (100g) firmly packed brown sugar
1/2 cup (125ml) treacle
1 egg yolk
2 1/2 cups (375g) plain flour
1 tablespoon ground ginger
1 teaspoon mixed spice
1 teaspoon bicarbonate of soda
Gold and silver cachous

ROYAL ICING
2 egg whites
3 cups (480g) pure icing sugar, approximately
Food colourings

Beat butter and sugar in small bowl with electric mixer until creamy; beat in treacle and egg yolk then stir in sifted dry ingredients. Knead dough on floured surface until smooth, cover; refrigerate 30 minutes. Roll out dough between sheets of baking paper until 4mm thick. Cut shapes from dough using Christmas biscuit cutters; cut a small hole in shapes for hanging, if desired. Place shapes 3cm apart on greased oven trays. Bake in moderate oven 10 minutes or until firm (time depends on the size of shapes). Transfer shapes to wire racks to cool. Spread or pipe Royal Icing onto shapes, decorate with cachous.

Royal Icing Beat egg whites in small bowl with electric mixer until just frothy; gradually beat in enough sifted icing sugar for mixture to form very stiff peaks. Divide icing into several small bowls; tint each bowl of icing with colouring as desired. Keep the surface of the icing covered with damp tea-towel to prevent it drying out.

Guaranteed spellbinders — gingerbread tree decorations make delicious treats for small visitors while the gingerbread house combines children's delight in all things miniature with their insatiable sweet-toothed appetites.

Plate: Wedgwood. Fabric: Laura Ashley.

Drinks

SPARKLING FRUITY PUNCH

MAKES ABOUT 6.5 LITRES (26 CUPS) SERVES 10

A non-alcoholic drink for those who like to get their "punch" from fruit juices. Refrigerate all ingredients before making the punch. Punch base can be prepared several hours ahead; add sparkling drinks just before serving.

2 litres (8 cups) orange and passionfruit juice drink
850ml can unsweetened pineapple juice
250g strawberries, chopped
1/4 cup (60ml) passionfruit pulp
2 medium (300g) red-skinned apples, chopped
2 medium (360g) oranges, peeled, chopped
1.25 litres (5 cups) lemon soda squash
1.25 litres (5 cups) creaming soda
3 cups (750ml) ginger beer
Fresh mint sprigs

Combine orange and passionfruit juice drink, pineapple juice and fruit in large bowl. Just before serving, stir in remaining ingredients. Serve cold.

ORANGE LIQUEUR FRAPPE

MAKES ABOUT 1 LITRE (4 CUPS) SERVES 6

The crushed ice required for this frappe can be made by wrapping ice cubes in a clean tea-towel and hitting them with a hammer. Recipe must be made just before serving.

1 cup (250ml) Cointreau
1 1/2 cups (375ml) orange juice, chilled
1 1/2 cups finely crushed ice

Combine Cointreau and juice in a large jug. Place 1/4 cup loosely packed ice into each of six 3/4 cup/180ml capacity serving glasses. Pour the liqueur mixture over ice; serve immediately.

COOL CHERRY COLA

MAKE ABOUT 750ML (3 CUPS) SERVES 4

While brandy-lemon base can be prepared several hours ahead, the cola should be added just before serving.

1 cup (250ml) cherry brandy
1 teaspoon lemon juice
Fresh lemon slices, halved
Whole cloves
Ice cubes
2 cups (500ml) cola

Combine cherry brandy and juice in large jug, cover; refrigerate for several hours. Stud lemon slices with cloves and use to decorate glasses, if desired. Just before serving, half-fill four 1 1/3 cups/330ml capacity serving glasses with ice cubes; top with combined cherry brandy mixture and cola.

COFFEE LIQUEUR EGGNOG

MAKES ABOUT 1.5 LITRES (6 CUPS) SERVES 8

While it is traditional to use brandy in eggnog, we have used Kahlua, a coffee-flavoured liqueur, in this version.

4 eggs, separated
1/3 cup (75g) caster sugar
2 cups (500ml) hot milk
2/3 cup (160ml) Kahlua
1/2 cup (125ml) cream

Place egg yolks, sugar and milk in large heat-proof bowl over a pan of simmering water; whisk about 15 minutes or until mixture lightly coats the back of a metal spoon. Remove from heat, stir in liqueur, cover; refrigerate 1 hour. Beat cream in small bowl until soft peaks form; fold into liqueur mixture. Beat egg whites in small bowl with electric mixer until soft peaks form; gently fold, in 2 batches, into liqueur mixture.

MULLED WINE (GLUHWEIN)

MAKES ABOUT 2 LITRES (8 CUPS)
SERVES 8 TO 10

A Christmas classic, mulled wine can be made 3 hours before serving.

2 litres (8 cups) red wine
3 cinnamon sticks
3 fresh orange slices
3 fresh lemon slices
8 whole cloves
1/3 cup (75g) caster sugar

Place all ingredients in large pan; stir over low heat for 20 minutes without boiling. Serve warm, or transfer to large bowl, cover; stand at room temperature for 3 hours.

Here's cheers! From left to right: *sparkling fruity punch; orange liqueur frappe; cool cherry cola; melon and orange punch; coffee liqueur eggnog; and mulled wine.*

Gift Ideas

Rosemary Cheese Wreaths

MAKES ABOUT 30

These savoury treats can be made 5 days ahead and stored in an airtight container.

1 cup (150g) plain flour
2 tablespoons self-raising flour
1/2 teaspoon hot paprika
125g butter
1 teaspoon caraway seeds
1/2 cup (60g) grated cheddar cheese
1/4 cup (20g) grated parmesan cheese
1 tablespoon water
1 tablespoon fresh rosemary leaves

Sift flours and paprika into medium bowl, rub in butter; stir in seeds, cheeses and water, mix to a soft dough. Knead dough on floured surface until smooth. Divide dough into 12 portions, roll each piece into 60cm log. Cut each log into 12cm lengths. Twist 2 lengths together; press ends together to form wreaths. Place about 2cm apart on greased oven trays; decorate with tiny sprigs of rosemary. Refrigerate 30 minutes. Bake in moderate oven about 20 minutes, or until browned lightly; cool on trays.

Panfortini

MAKES 10

Traditional treats from Italy, these tiny versions of panforte can be made a month ahead and stored at room temperature in an airtight container, or frozen up to 3 months.

2 sheets (15cm x 24cm) edible rice paper
1/2 cup (75g) macadamias, toasted, chopped
3/4 cup (120g) blanched almonds, toasted, chopped
1 cup (100g) walnuts, toasted, chopped
1/2 cup (85g) mixed peel
1/3 cup (85g) chopped glace peaches
1/4 cup (60g) chopped glace figs
1/4 cup (25g) cocoa powder
1/2 cup (75g) plain flour
1 teaspoon ground cinnamon
1 teaspoon mixed spice
1/2 cup (125ml) honey
1/3 cup (75g) caster sugar
2 tablespoons icing sugar mixture
1/2 teaspoon ground cinnamon, extra

Grease ten 7.5cm egg rings. Cut circles from rice paper to fit inside rings; place rings with rice paper on oven trays. Combine nuts, fruit and sifted cocoa, flour and spices in large bowl; mix well. Combine honey and caster sugar in small heavy-based pan; stir over low heat, without boiling, until sugar dissolves. Bring to boil; boil, uncovered, without stirring, about 2 minutes or until syrup reaches soft ball stage (115°C) on a candy thermometer (or when a teaspoon of syrup dropped into a cup of cold water moulds easily with fingers into a soft ball). Add hot syrup to fruit and nut mixture; mix well. Firmly press 1/4 cup of mixture into each prepared ring. Bake in moderately slow oven about 20 minutes or until just firm; cool in rings. Run a knife around edges of rings to remove. Dust with combined sifted icing sugar and extra cinnamon before serving.

Chocolate Hazelnut Biscotti

MAKES ABOUT 28

Another Italian treat, biscotti can be made a week ahead and stored at room temperature in an airtight container, or you can freeze un-iced biscotti for 3 months.

1 1/4 cups (185g) hazelnuts
3 eggs, beaten lightly
1/2 cup (100g) firmly packed brown sugar
1/2 cup (110g) caster sugar
1 1/4 cups (185g) plain flour
3/4 cup (110g) self-raising flour
1/3 cup (35g) cocoa powder
1 teaspoon ground ginger
1 teaspoon instant coffee powder
1 teaspoon vanilla essence
2 tablespoons Irish Cream liqueur
100g dark chocolate, grated finely
200g dark chocolate, melted, extra

Spread nuts in single layer on oven tray, bake in moderate oven about 5 minutes or until skins begin to split. Rub the nuts briskly in a tea-towel to remove skins.

Beat eggs and sugars in medium bowl with electric mixer until smooth and changed in colour. Stir in sifted dry ingredients, essence, liqueur, grated chocolate and nuts; mix to a firm dough. Gently knead dough on floured surface until smooth; place on greased large oven tray, shape into 14cm x 28cm log. Bake, uncovered, in moderate oven about 1 hour or until firm. Cool on tray 10 minutes. Using serrated knife, cut log on an angle into 1cm slices. Place slices close together on oven trays, bake in moderate oven 15 minutes or until both sides are dry and crisp; cool. If desired, spread one side of each biscotti with extra chocolate, allow to set at room temperature.

A batch of delicious treats from your kitchen is great to have in reserve for those last-minute presents or for the person who doesn't want any more socks or notepaper. On this page, rosemary cheese wreaths and, opposite, panfortini and chocolate hazelnut biscotti.

SUGARED ALMONDS

MAKES ABOUT 1½ CUPS

Similar to Vienna almonds, these sugared nuts are simply irresistible; they can be kept, in an airtight container, in a cool, dry place for 2 weeks.

½ cup (110g) caster sugar
¼ cup (60ml) water
1½ cups (240g) blanched almonds
30g butter

Combine sugar and water in medium heavy-based pan; stir over heat, without boiling, until sugar dissolves. Simmer, uncovered, without stirring, until temperature reaches soft ball stage (115°C) on a candy thermometer (or when a teaspoon of syrup dropped into a cup of cold water moulds easily with fingers into a soft ball).

Remove from heat, stir in almonds; stir until mixture crystallises. Return pan to heat; stir over low heat for about 5 minutes or until almonds turn golden and are coated with the caramel. Add butter, stir until melted. Turn almonds onto large oven tray. Separate almonds, using two forks, while still hot.

MINI TRUFFLE PUDDINGS

MAKES ABOUT 20

Recipe can be made 4 days ahead; keep, covered, under refrigeration.

3 cups (300g) plain cake crumbs
¼ cup (25g) cocoa powder
¼ cup (60ml) apricot jam, warmed, sieved
2 tablespoons dark underproof rum
1 tablespoon water
1 tablespoon apricot jam, warmed, sieved, extra
½ cup (50g) chocolate sprinkles
4 green glace cherries
180g white chocolate, melted
4 red glace cherries, chopped

Combine crumbs with sifted cocoa in large bowl; stir in combined jam, rum and water, mix well. Roll level tablespoons of mixture into balls; brush lightly with extra jam, roll in sprinkles. Place on tray, cover, refrigerate until firm.

Place puddings in mini truffle cases. Cut green cherries in half; cut each half into thin wedges. Drizzle tops of truffles with white chocolate. Decorate with red and green cherries.

Opposite, more food for thought or, more exactly, thoughtfulness — florentines, sugared almonds and mini truffle puddings.

FLORENTINES

MAKES ABOUT 35

Mouthwatering florentines can be made a month ahead and stored in an airtight container in refrigerator.

2 cups (60g) cornflakes
½ cup (80g) sultanas
¼ cup (35g) dried currants
¼ cup (60g) chopped red glace cherries
¼ cup (60g) chopped green glace cherries
¾ cup (105g) slivered almonds, toasted
¾ cup (180ml) sweetened condensed milk
200g dark chocolate, melted

Combine cornflakes, fruit, nuts and condensed milk in large bowl; mix well. Drop level tablespoons of mixture about 4cm apart on oven trays covered with baking paper. Bake in moderate oven about 8 minutes or until browned lightly; cool on trays. Spread bases of florentines with chocolate; make wavy lines in chocolate with fork just before chocolate sets.

Spiced fruit and nuts, below, an exotic mix that is easily prepared.

SPICED FRUIT AND NUT MIX

MAKES ABOUT 5 CUPS

Give this mix in tins or jars which you've decorated yourself. It can be made a week ahead and stored in an airtight container.

2 tablespoons olive oil
1 cup (160g) blanched almonds
1 tablespoon ground cumin
1 tablespoon ground coriander
1 teaspoon hot paprika
½ teaspoon ground turmeric
1 egg white
1½ tablespoons lemon juice
⅔ cup (100g) chopped dried apricots
½ cup (80g) sultanas
½ cup (80g) seeded chopped dates
2 cups (300g) roasted unsalted cashews

Heat oil in pan; add almonds, cook, stirring, until browned lightly. Add spices, cook, stirring, until fragrant. Whisk egg white in large bowl until frothy, stir in spice mixture and remaining ingredients. Spread mixture onto greased oven tray. Bake, uncovered, in moderate oven about 20 minutes or until mixture is dry and crisp, stirring occasionally; cool.

Deck the Halls

Ever since Prince Albert set up a decorated fir at Windsor Castle in 1861, the tree has taken centre stage during the Christmas festivities — it seems that no amount of repetition can dull the pleasure of setting it up and decking it out. And once the tree's looking good, there's the mantelpiece and front door to decorate, the stockings to make, and the table settings to consider ...

Bright and Simple

A richly decorated tree can be achieved for a very small outlay, while giving the impression of no expense spared. Using metallic card and sequins, scissors and glue, we show you how to put the glamour back into Christmas.

FOLDED STAR

MATERIALS
Metallic card
Tracing paper
Pencil and ruler
Scissors
Metal skewer
Fine gold or silver cord

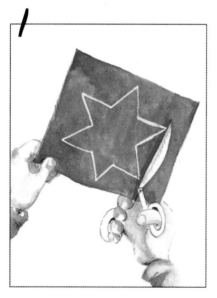

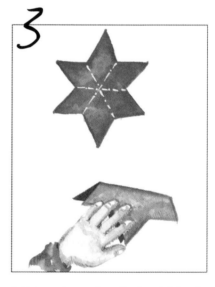

Trace the outline of the six-pointed star printed on the pattern sheet onto the wrong side of the metallic card, and cut out (**Pic 1**).

Mark the lines joining the points, then fold *away* from you along these lines, crease firmly and open out again (**Pic 2**). You might need to score along the lines before folding.

Fold *towards* you along the lines joining the angles, crease firmly and open out again (**Pic 3**). The star should now bend easily into its 3-D shape. Using the metal skewer, make a hole in the top or the centre of the star and thread through the gold or silver cord, for hanging.

3-D BAUBLES

MATERIALS
**Double-sided metallic card, or card-
board and foil wrapping paper**
Pencil and ruler
Scissors
Glittery curling ribbon
Sequins
Craft glue or glue stick

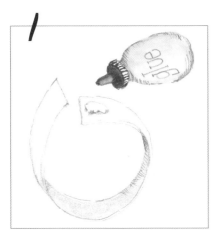

Cut the double-sided card into 2cm x 22cm
strips. Glue the ends of each strip together to
form a ring (**Pic 1**). If you cannot find double-
sided metallic card, use ordinary cardboard and
cover the rings with foil wrapping paper, gluing
on the inside.

For each bauble, push one ring inside another so
that they are at right angles (**Pic 2**).

Tie a froth of glittery curling ribbon at the top of
each bauble and add a piece long enough for
tying to the tree. Glue on sequins to the bauble to
add extra sparkle (**Pic 3**).

PAPER CHAINS

MATERIALS
Wrapping paper
Pencil and ruler
Scissors
Craft glue or glue stick

Cut the paper into 1.5cm x 14cm strips (**Pic 1**).

Glue one strip to itself to make the first link in
the chain (**Pic 2**). If using craft glue, use it spar-
ingly — a small dob only is needed.

Thread another strip through the first and glue
it to itself for the second link, and so on and so
on and so on ... (**Pic 3**)

For a paper chain with a twist, use double-
sided paper or glue two different-coloured papers
back to back so that both sides of the chain links
are decorative. Twist each link to display each
colour.

Plaited Hearts

MATERIALS

Metallic card in two different colours
Tracing paper
Pencil and ruler
Scissors
Craft glue
Metal skewer
Narrow ribbon or fine metallic cord

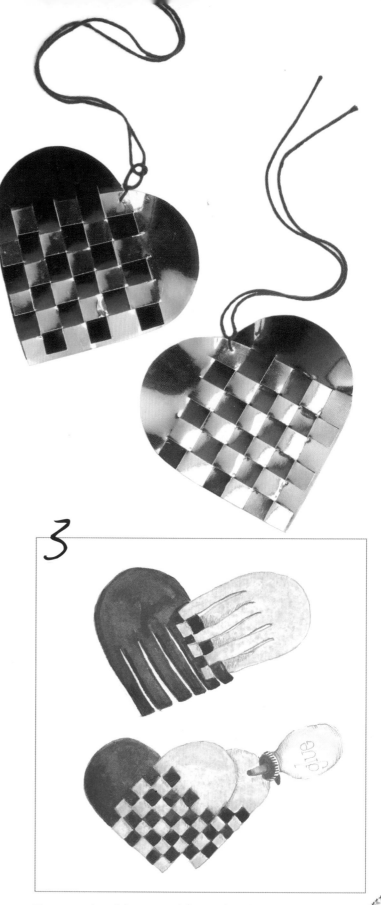

Trace the shape printed on the pattern sheet four times onto the back of the two different-coloured metallic cards — twice onto one colour and twice onto the other. Mark the dotted lines (**Pic 1**).

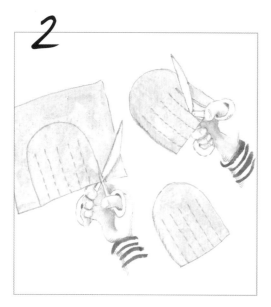

Cut out the four shapes, then cut along the dotted lines on each (**Pic 2**).

Weave one coloured shape into a different-coloured shape. Make two hearts in this way, then glue the hearts together (**Pic 3**).

Trim the edges of the heart to neaten. Use the skewer to make a hole in the top, just below the V of the heart. Thread ribbon or cord through this for attaching to the tree.

STRING OF STARS

MATERIALS

Foil wrapping paper or tissue paper
Tracing paper
Pencil and ruler
Scissors
Craft glue (if joining strips)
Glitter and spray adhesive (optional)

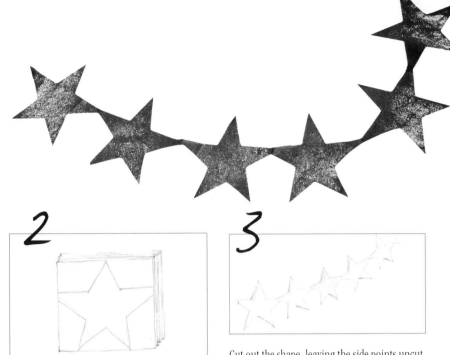

Concertina fold a 10cm x 90cm strip of tissue paper or foil into 10cm squares (**Pic 1**).

Trace the simple five-pointed star shape printed on the pattern sheet onto the top square; make sure the two cut-off side points reach right out to the sides (**Pic 2**).

Cut out the shape, leaving the side points uncut. When you open out the strip you'll have a row of stars joined at two points (**Pic 3**). Glue other strips to this one for a longer tree decoration. Decorate with glitter, if desired.

SEQUIN BAUBLES

Note that pinned sequins can be dangerous for young children, so hang these ornaments where they cannot be grasped by small hands

MATERIALS

For each bauble:
Polystyrene ball, 23cm circumference
One packet silver sequins
One packet pearly sequins
Craft pins
Pearl-headed pins
String of pearls or tiny silver baubles
Darning needle or metal skewer
Craft glue

Pencil a line around the centre of the ball, then divide it into six equal segments. Extend one pencil mark up by 2cm, then extend the next mark down by 2cm. Continue around the ball in this fashion until you have three marks above the centre and three below. Now join the dots to create a wave pattern around the ball (**Pic 1**).

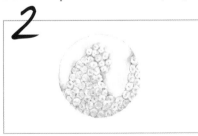

Using the craft pins, pin silver sequins below the wave line and pearly sequins above the wave line. Attach some sequins using the pearl-headed pins (**Pic 2**).

Using craft pins, attach a string of pearls or tiny silver baubles, following the wave line.

Make a hole at the top of the ball with the skewer and squeeze some glue into it. Make a loop of the string of pearls or tiny baubles and squeeze the ends into the hole (**Pic 3**).

You can make your sequin baubles as simple or as elaborate as you like. For a classic look, pin silver sequins all over the ball, studding with pearl-headed pins at intervals. For a more baroque look, glue on lengths of silver ribbon, and decorate with pearl-headed pins.

Double Star

MATERIALS
Double-sided metallic card
Tracing paper
Pencil and ruler
Scissors
Sticky tape
Metal skewer
Fine silver or gold cord

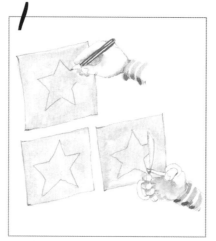

Trace two outlines of the five-pointed star printed on the pattern sheet onto metallic card, and cut out to make two matching stars (**Pic 1**).

Mark where the centre falls on each star. On one star, draw a line from any one point to the centre. On the other star, mark from an angle to the centre, as shown. Cut the stars along these lines (**Pic 2**).

Slot one star into the other and, if necessary, hold both together with sticky tape (**Pic 3**).

Use the skewer to make a hole in one of the points and thread cord through the hole so that you can hang your star.

ANGELS

MATERIALS

Silver or gold metallic card
Large dinner plate or compass
Pencil
Scissors
White crêpe paper
White tissue paper
Silver or gold tissue paper,
    or silver or gold
    foil wrapping paper
Silver or gold twisted
    paper ribbon
Twist of silver or gold
    curling ribbon,
    about 8cm long
Silver or gold stars
Fast-setting craft glue
Sticky tape
Fine silver or gold cord

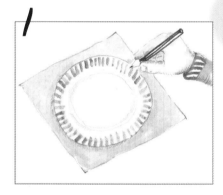

Draw a circle, at least 30cm in diameter, on the silver or gold card. The quickest way is to trace a large dinner plate, but you can also use a compass. Divide the circle into quarters and cut out — you'll get four angels from this one circle (**Pic 1**).

Run a thin line of glue down one straight side of card, then fold over onto other straight side to form a cone. Hold in place until glue is set. Snip off about 2cm at the top of the cone (**Pic 2**).

Cut out a 14cm square from white crêpe and fill with tissue paper or waste crêpe to make a head shape (**Pic 3**). Glue silver or gold tissue paper or foil over head to cover. Push the head into the top of the cone and tape it on the inside.

These cornucopias are really just upside-down angels — minus the head and wings. Make the cones from metallic paper, following the instructions for the angels, decorate with stars, then glue a hanging cord to either side of the open ends. Line with tissue paper, fill with sweets and hang from the tree.

Unravel the twisted paper ribbon and form into a bow shape, securing with the silver or gold cord, for the wings. Glue to the angel's back (**Pic 4**).

Glue a piece of curling ribbon to the head, for the halo, then glue on a silver or gold hanging cord. Decorate the cone with stars.

Country Christmas

With the aid of humble biscuit cutters, you can bring the warmth and simplicity of country style to your Christmas decorations. Gingerbread men and other traditional shapes, in both bread dough and fabric, are combined on a tree with simple fabric-wrapped balls for a Christmas style that's as welcoming as a country kitchen.

BREAD DOUGH DECORATIONS

MATERIALS

1 cup cooking salt
1 cup warm water
2 teaspoons cooking oil or glycerine
3 cups plain flour
Gingerbread cutters in desired shapes
Sewing needle and skewer
1 tablespoon instant coffee
1/3 cup boiling water
Aluminium foil
Fine sandpaper
Estapol Matt varnish
Fine cord or string

Dissolve the salt in warm water, mix in oil or glycerine. Mix this liquid into flour. Turn the dough onto a floured surface and knead until pliable and plastic-like in appearance. Keep in an air-tight container. Break off pieces as required.

Roll out the dough and cut shapes with cutters. Prick each all over with a sewing needle to prevent pastry puffing up, and make a hole in each piece with a skewer, for hanging thread.

For an antique look, glaze before baking with instant coffee mixed in boiling water, and check while cooking to see whether more glaze is needed.

Cover a baking tray with aluminium foil, dull side up. Place the decorations on the foil, and bake on the bottom shelf of the oven on the lowest temperature setting (100–150°C, or 210–300°F) until hard (1 1/2–2 hours).

When completely cool, lightly sand the edges of the dough to reveal a lighter colour and varnish with Estapol Matt (this will preserve the dough from insect invasion or mould).

Attach a hanging thread.

COUNTRY FABRIC DECORATIONS

MATERIALS

Scraps of country fabric
Gingerbread cutters in desired shapes
Fusible Fleece
Buttons, beads and ribbon, to trim

Trace around cutters directly onto fabric (**Pic 1**), adding an extra 5mm all around for seam allowance when cutting.

For each shape, cut two fabric pieces with seam allowance and one Fusible Fleece piece without seam allowance. With right sides facing, sew fabric pieces together, leaving a small opening. Iron Fusible Fleece onto one side of shape (**Pic 2**).

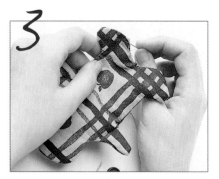

Turn right side out, enclosing Fleece. Slipstitch opening closed (**Pic 3**), and decorate padded shape as desired, with bow, beads, button eyes and so on. Attach a hanging thread.

SPICY SANTAS

MATERIALS

1 large cinnamon stick
2 small cinnamon sticks
Red and white paint
Red ribbon
Small white pompom
PVA glue

Children will enjoy making these spicy Santas, which can be used to trim the Christmas tree, parcels or even napkin rings. Paint a hat, beard and face on the large cinnamon stick for the body, then paint red and white cuffs on one end of each of the small cinnamon sticks for the arms. Glue the arms to the body, then glue the ends of the ribbon, tucked under the pompom, to the hat, forming a hanging loop.

WRAPPED CHRISTMAS BALLS

MATERIALS

Scraps of country fabric
Polystyrene balls of different sizes
PVA glue

For larger balls, cut fabric into 2cm-wide strips. Strips for smaller balls can be 1–1.5cm wide. Use PVA glue to anchor each strip at the start.

Wrap the first strip around the ball, like wool, and glue the end to finish. Continue adding strips until the ball is covered. Add a hanging loop if desired.

All the family can be drafted to assist with these decorations — younger members can help with cutting and decorating bread dough, while steadier hands might be needed for the fabric ornaments.

Add strips of fabric ties to the biscuit cutters themselves and hang them on the tree as well.

From the Garden

Happily, there can be much more to Christmas greenery than the Christmas tree ... garlands, wreaths and floral centrepieces are all part of the Christmas tradition. They're high on impact, yet a breeze to make, especially if you follow our directions.

For a resilient decoration, use long-lasting evergreen material — conifers such as pine, spruce and cypress, glossy-leafed plants such as camellia, privet, Magnolia grandiflora, *holly, fig and gardenia, and dry climate plants such as eucalyptus, protea and banksia. If berries are in season, use cotoneaster, berberis and hips of hawthorn and rose. Creepers and climbers such as ivy, of course, and hops are indispensable.*

EASY GARLAND

MATERIALS

Ball of string
Cardboard cut into spool shape
Suitable greenery
Secateurs

Measure the area you want to garland, allowing extra for soft draping and for tying while constructing the garland. Cut two lengths of string generously to measure. Wind one length of string around a cardboard spool — it makes the string easier to manage (**Pic 1**).

You need to keep the other length of string reasonably taut while constructing the garland; tie it between two chairs across the top of a table (as shown) or between verandah posts. If you haven't space to construct the whole garland in one piece, make smaller garlands and join them together. Tie one end of the spooled string to the first chair back as well.

Take a good thick bunch of plant material and bind it, not too tightly, to the taut string with the spooled string (**Pic 2**).

Keep adding plant material in good thick quantities as you work along the string. It's as simple as that. Work to the end and tie off the spooled string.

To cover any bald or skinny spots or to give your garland a more substantial girth, tuck in extra plant material, catching it a couple of times under the bound string or creepers (**Pic 3**). Knot both ends of string together at each end and trim. You may also wish to continue adding greenery or flowers to the garland when it is hung in place.

TABLE CENTREPIECE

MATERIALS

Fresh Oasis brick

Florist's tray to fit brick (or a leftover
    take-away food tray)

Florist tape

Plain white candles, 25–30cm high

Three oranges

Three limes

Lino cutter, to score fruit

Whole cloves

Florist wire, heavy and light gauge

Approximately 4m x 2cm-wide wired
    organza ribbon

Fresh greenery

Cedar roses or other pods

Sprigs of privet berries or similar

Gold spray paint

Cinnamon sticks

Dried orange slices (see box)

Glue gun

Use florist tape to secure the Oasis brick to the tray. Soak brick in water, for at least 15 minutes or until thoroughly wet. Trim candles to different heights and insert in brick (**Pic 1**).

To make pomander citrus, use the lino cutter to score the oranges and limes in desired pattern, and press cloves into the cuts. Pass a length of heavy gauge wire through the base of the oranges and limes, fold down the protruding ends and press firmly into the Oasis (**Pic 2**).

Cut wired ribbon into short lengths, each about 40cm. Form each length into a couple of loops, tie at the base with light gauge florist wire, and push into the Oasis (**Pic 3**).

TO DRY ORANGE SLICES

Cut an orange into thin slices. Blot with paper towel to soak up excess juice. Place slices on baking sheets lined with baking paper, and place in very cool oven (it's even a good idea to use a tea-towel to keep oven door slightly ajar). Turn slices every half hour or so to dry evenly. Slices could take 4–6 hours to dry. Leave to cool. The dried slices can be used as is or sprayed with gloss varnish to preserve for a dried arrangement.

Cut greenery into short lengths and push into the Oasis at even intervals to create a framework of the desired shape for the arrangement. Wire cedar roses and sprigs of greenery together (using light gauge wire) and push these sprigs into the Oasis (**Pic 4**).

Spray sprigs of berries with gold paint and leave to dry. Push sprigs of berries and cinnamon sticks into the arrangement, and use a glue gun to attach dried orange slices (**Pic 5**).

CITRUS WREATH

MATERIALS

Fresh Oasis wreath
  (set in plastic ring — see Pic 1)
Florist wire, heavy and light gauge
Fresh greenery of choice
Secateurs
Cinnamon sticks
Sprigs of privet berries or similar

Gold spray paint
Approximately 4m x 2cm-wide wired
  organza ribbon
Kumquats or faux citrus fruits
Dried orange slices (see box, p. 64)
Nuts, cedar roses or seed pods
Glue gun

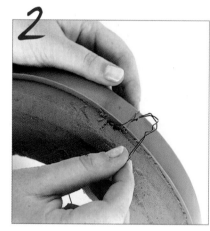

Pass a piece of heavy gauge florist wire through the Oasis and fold around the back of the wreath (**Pic 2**). Twist wire into a loop for hanging, trim the ends. Cut sharp edge from the Oasis wreath using a kitchen knife. Soak Oasis in water for at least 15 minutes or until wet through.

Cut greenery into short lengths and push in at even intervals around the inner and outer circle of wreath. Push cinnamon sticks in at intervals around the wreath or use a short piece of light gauge florist wire bent into a "U" shape to hold them in place (**Pic 3**).

For a simple and stylish napkin trim, wrap a stem of ivy or other greenery around each napkin, tie with florist wire and add a couple of gold-painted leaves and a sprig of berries.

Spray sprigs of berries with gold paint and leave to dry. Insert sprayed berries at intervals around the wreath. Cut wired ribbon into short lengths, each about 40cm. Form each length into a couple of loops, and tie at base with light gauge wire. Push loops into the arrangement (**Pic 4**).

If using real fruit, push a length of heavy gauge wire through the base of the fruit, fold down protruding ends and push into wreath. If using faux fruit, use a glue gun to attach to surrounding foliage (**Pic 5**). Arrange dried orange slices among fruit and foliage, and keep in place using glue gun or wire "pins". Fill spaces with nuts or pods, extra foliage and berries.

Shelf Life

Once you've loaded up the tree, you can turn your attention to the mantelpiece. By this stage, it's probably in need of a spot of Christmas cheer. The kids can get busy making the Santas and carollers, which will provide them with plenty of decorating opportunities. These easy-to-make characters require no special purchases, as they are good consumers of recycled materials; they'll use up toilet rolls and scraps of paper, and those annoying socks without partners. In the meantime, adults can take a turn on the sewing machine, whipping up an inimitable twosome called Dave and Celeste. Instructions begin on page 71.

Your Santas can be trimmed lavishly or with restraint. Our gold Santa falls into the unrestrained category — his robe has been decorated with gold braid and his hands painted gold to match his golden demeanour. If, after trimming, you still feel there's room for something extra, glue on some glitter, to finish.

Santas and Carollers

SANTAS

MEASUREMENTS

Finished Santas range from 24cm to 33cm high, including hats.

MATERIALS

**Thin cardboard, or cardboard tube
    from roll of plastic wrap**

**Pink, red, white, black and gold
    acrylic paints**

Flat brush and fine liner brush

Red crêpe paper

Gold paper (if making gold Santa)

Sewing cotton

**Cottonwool or fake fur fabric, gold
    braid or cord, bells, black satin
    ribbon, craft foam, gold pompoms,
    plastic holly, and glitter and spray
    adhesive (optional), for trims**

Craft glue

Scalpel or craft knife

Cut down a cardboard tube from a roll of plastic wrap to desired length. If using cardboard, cut a rectangle approximately 17cm wide x desired length, then roll this piece of card to form a tube, overlapping 1.5cm, and glue to hold.

If you can't lay your hands on odd socks for the carollers' hats, make paper ones from crêpe paper, as for the Santas.

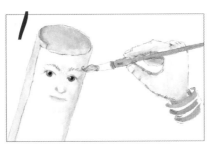

Brush on a layer of pink paint all over the tube, allow to dry. Using the liner brush and red, white and black acrylics, paint on a simple face (**Pic 1**).

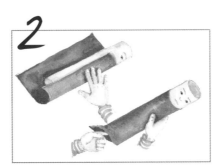

From red crêpe or gold paper, cut a rectangle that wraps around the tube with some overlap and is the same length as the tube, for robe. Cut another rectangle to same width and about 17cm long, for hat. Wrap and glue the robe piece around the tube, leaving face exposed and excess extending at base. Tuck excess up into the tube (**Pic 2**).

Wrap and glue hat piece around top of Santa's head. Tie free end with sewing cotton.

Now you come to the fun part: decorating your Santa. We glued cottonwool or fake fur fabric around the base of the hat and the robe, down the centre front of the robe, and onto the lower part of the face, for a beard. Our gold Santa is trimmed with gold braid or cord, while one of the traditional red Santas sports a strip of black satin ribbon around the waist. We cut rough hand shapes and a bell holder from craft foam using a craft knife or scalpel, then glued a hand on each side of centre trim, emerging from cottonwool sleeve trims. The bell holder, with bell attached, was glued to one of the hands. The hat can be trimmed with a pompom or a bunch of holly.

CAROLLERS

MEASUREMENTS

Each finished caroller is approximately 18cm high, including hat.

MATERIALS

**Thin cardboard, or cardboard tube
    from toilet roll**

Pink acrylic paint

Flat brush

Fine black marker pen

Green and red crêpe paper

Glittery ribbon

Old socks in bright colours, for hats

Sewing cotton

Tissue paper

Small gold bells and glitter, for trims

Craft glue

You'll need one toilet roll per caroller. If using cardboard, cut a rectangle, 17cm x 10cm, then roll this piece of card to form a tube, overlapping 1.5cm, and glue to secure.

Brush on a layer of pink paint all over the tube, allow to dry. Draw on simple eyes and mouth, using fine black marker pen

From green crêpe paper, cut a rectangle, 34cm x 10cm, and from red crêpe, cut a rectangle, 34cm x 5.5cm. Wrap and glue green crêpe around tube, tucking excess extending at base up into tube. Wrap and glue red crêpe around top of green crêpe, leaving face exposed. Glue and tie ribbon around top of crêpe paper, for scarf.

Cut the toe off a sock, then wind cotton around the cut-off end. Stuff with scrunched tissue paper and place on the caroller's head.

Decorate your carollers however you like — we painted pink blobs for hands, glued on a little bell and added dots of glitter, for buttons.

Dave and Celeste

Meet Dave and his angelic partner, Celeste. Once these two have spent a festive season perched disarmingly on the mantelpiece, offering their own particular brand of whimsical humour, it will be hard to imagine Christmas without them. Never mind that red-nosed Dave obviously likes a glass or two and the slightly bewildered Celeste sometimes thinks she's a fairy — they'd make even Scrooge smile and it's Christmas, after all.

DAVE THE REINDEER

MEASUREMENTS

Dave is approximately 37cm high, including his antlers.

MATERIALS

0.5m x 112cm calico
Teabags, optional (see Note, below)
Polyester filling
Raffia
Metallic gold machine thread
Two pieces firm wire, each 20cm long
Kitty litter (gravel type)
Fine brown fabric pen
Blusher or red pencil
2cm-diameter self-cover button
Scrap of red fabric, for button
Small gold bell

Note: If you wish to tea-dye your calico, make a strong solution of boiling tea, using three or four teabags, immerse calico until tea is cold, dry the fabric, press and proceed.

All pattern pieces are printed on the pattern sheet. Trace head/body, base, leg and arm (**Pic 1**). 5mm seam allowance is **included** on all pattern pieces.

From calico, cut two heads/bodies, one base, four legs and four arms.

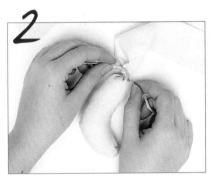

With right sides facing, stitch legs together in pairs, leaving the top edge open. Clip curves and turn right side out. Fill feet firmly with polyester filling as far as the given line, and tie securely with raffia to keep stuffing in place (**Pic 2**).

With right sides facing, stitch arms together in pairs, leaving top edge open. Clip curves, turn right side out, fill with polyester filling and tie off, as for legs.

Using double thread, run a line of gathering stitch across tops of arms and legs, as indicated on pattern, through both layers. Pull up gathers tightly on arms and tie off securely (**Pic 3**). Do not pull up gathers on legs.

With right sides facing, stitch head/body sections together, leaving lower edge open. Clip curves, especially around antlers, and turn head/body right side out.

Stitch antlers, following stitching lines on pattern and using metallic gold thread. Insert a piece of wire into each antler, between stitching lines, then stitch across base of each antler by hand (**Pic 4**). Do not stitch these lines by machine, as each wire should extend beyond antler into head and could damage your needle.

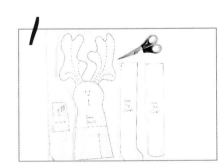

With right sides together and raw edges matching, position legs on lower edge of front body, draw up gathers slightly to fit, then baste legs in place (**Pic 5**).

With right sides together, stitch base to body at front and sides, leaving back edge open for filling. Fill upper head/body with polyester filling as far as line indicated on pattern, then fill lower body with kitty litter (**Pic 6**). (The litter is to weight Dave's lower body so that he sits securely.) Turn in remaining raw edges of body and base and close with ladder stitch.

Continued over page

Stitch arms to body at sides, in the positions marked on pattern, leaving upper raw edges exposed above gathering (**Pic 7**). The raw edges will be covered by the raffia tie.

Following pattern markings, draw face with fabric pen and add a little blusher or red pencil to cheeks. Cover button with red fabric and stitch to centre of face. Tie a large raffia bow around Dave's neck and add a gold bell (**Pic 8**).

Emerging out of calico and kitty litter, Dave the reindeer and Celeste the angel are unfazed by their humble origins. In fact, their rustic simplicity is the key to their appeal. And they're meant to look slightly dishevelled, so there's no need to strive for perfect stitching.

CELESTE THE ANGEL

MEASUREMENTS
Celeste sits approximately 15.5cm high, excluding her wings.

MATERIALS
0.25m x 112cm calico
Polyester filling
Kitty litter (gravel type)
Gold metallic machine thread
Small amount raffia
0.5m x 4cm-wide wire-edged ribbon, for wings
Fine brown fabric pen
Blusher or red pencil
Small piece gold tinsel
7cm twig, for wand
Gold paint (optional)
Small gold sequin star
Glue gun or craft glue

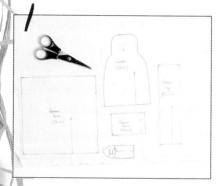

All pattern pieces are printed on the pattern sheet. Trace head/body, base, arm, leg and dress (**Pic 1**). 5mm seam allowance is **included** on all pieces.

From calico, cut two heads/bodies, one base, four arms, two legs and two dresses.

Fold legs in half lengthwise, right sides together, and stitch long seam. With seam at centre back, stitch across one short edge. Trim corners, turn right side out. Fill each leg firmly for about 7cm from bottom, leaving upper leg unstuffed (**Pic 2**).

3

With right sides facing, stitch head/body sections together, leaving lower edge open. Clip curves, turn right side out. With right sides facing and matching raw edges, baste legs to lower edge of front body (**Pic 3**).

4

With right sides together, stitch base to body at front and sides, leaving back edge open. Fill head and half of body with polyester filling, then fill lower half of body with kitty litter (**Pic 4**).

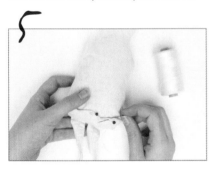

5

Turn in remaining raw edge of body and base and close with ladder stitch (**Pic 5**).

6

With right sides facing, stitch arms together in pairs, leaving top edge open. Clip curves, turn right side out and fill with polyester, leaving top 3cm of each arm unfilled. With right sides facing and raw edges even, baste arms to each side of one dress section, as indicated on pattern (**Pic 6**).

7

With right sides facing, stitch dress sections together at sides, sandwiching arms at the same time. Using gold machine thread, finish upper and lower edges of dress with simple zigzag. Thread a strand of raffia into a large-eyed needle and hand-sew a line of gathering stitches around neck edge of dress, starting and finishing at centre front (**Pic 7**).

8

Place dress onto angel and draw up gathers firmly around neck, tying raffia ends in a bow at centre front.

Following pattern markings, draw a rudimentary face on angel and add blusher or red pencil to cheeks. Glue a little gold tinsel to head for hair.

Tie wire-edged ribbon into a large bow, trim the ends evenly and stitch to the back of the dress, bending the loops into position as wings.

Paint twig gold, if desired, and glue a small gold star to one end. Glue the stick between the angel's hands (**Pic 8**).

Table Manners

These elegant table settings will do the most elaborate Christmas dinner justice. Featuring festive colours and traditional Christmas motifs, and containing all the good cheer of the season, they are quick and easy to create with the aid of our cover stencil.

STENCILLED PLACEMATS

MEASUREMENTS

Each finished placemat measures 27cm x 34cm.

MATERIALS

- **30cm x 35cm each of red and white felt, for one placemat**
- **Rotary cutter with straight-edged and wavy-edged blades, or scissors and pinking shears**
- **Self-healing cutting mat**
- **Ruler**
- **Large and small star stencils on the cover**
- **Craft knife or scalpel**
- **Masking tape**
- **Magic Tape**
- **Silver acrylic paint**
- **Fabric medium**
- **Stencil brush or natural sponge**
- **Paper towel**
- **Fusible webbing**
- **Stranded embroidery cotton, red**
- **Embroidery needle**

Using the straight-edged blade on the rotary cutter or a pair of scissors, from the red felt, cut required number of rectangles (one per placemat), each 27cm x 34cm. Measure and mark 3cm down each side from one corner, join the marks and cut along the line to remove corner. Repeat for remaining corners.

Using the wavy-edged blade on the rotary cutter or pinking shears, from the white felt, cut the same number of rectangles, each 23cm x 30cm. Mark and measure 2cm down each side from a corner, join the marks and cut along the line to remove the corner. Repeat for remaining corners.

We stencilled a few large and small silver stars over the white felt.

To prepare stencil, remove stars from surrounding plastic, using a craft knife or scalpel to cut across attaching tabs so that stars come cleanly away. Do not attempt to push the stencil out without cutting first — this could result in ragged edges or tears that would spoil your work.

Use masking tape to cover the parts of the stencil you don't want to use. Position stencil on a white felt piece and hold in place with a strip of Magic Tape along one side. Mix acrylic paint with fabric medium according to manufacturer's instructions. Dip brush or sponge into mixture, and pounce out excess paint onto a paper towel. When brush or sponge is nearly dry, apply paint to the stencil, pouncing the brush and aiming to achieve an even coverage. Remove stencil, wipe dry, then begin again on another part of the felt (**Pic 1**). Allow to dry, then heat-set by ironing.

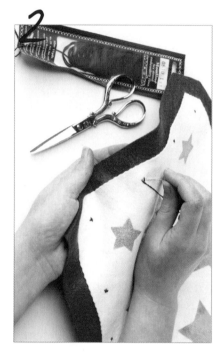

Cut the fusible webbing into 10cm-wide strips. Place strips, paper side up, on red felt piece, and iron to fuse in place. Remove backing paper, then centre the stencilled white felt piece on the red felt piece with the strips of fusible webbing sandwiched in between, iron in place.

Using three strands of embroidery cotton, work a small cross-stitch in each corner and a few along the edges of the white felt, about 1.5cm from the edge (**Pic 2**).

To continue the starry theme, stencil some paper napkins to match.

These made-in-minutes felt placemats show one way to use the stencil on the cover. But if there's too little time to make even the mats, don't overlook adding your own touch to paper napkins.

HOLLY TABLECLOTH

MEASUREMENTS
Our cloth measures 175cm x 250cm.

MATERIALS

Single white cotton bedsheet

White cotton napkins

Tape measure and pins

Stencil on cover

Craft knife or scalpel

Masking tape

Magic Tape

Deep green and red acrylic paint

Fabric medium (optional)

Two stencil brushes

Paper towel

Wash the sheet and napkins in warm soapy water and rinse well without fabric softener. Iron flat.

Use pins to mark a border strip about 17cm wide around the edges of the sheet. Beginning about 30cm from each corner, measure and mark equal intervals along the border strip to indicate placement of holly sprigs (refer to the photograph, opposite), remembering to leave space for the berries in between.

Prepare the stencil by carefully removing the berries and leaves, using a craft knife or scalpel. Cover the berries on the stencil with masking tape in preparation for stencilling the leaves. Place a piece of paper or cardboard under the area of the cloth to be stencilled first. Place the stencil in position, and hold in place with a strip of Magic Tape along one side. Mix the green acrylic paint with fabric medium according to the manufacturer's instructions, or use the green fabric paint undiluted. Load a stencil brush with the paint, and pounce the loaded brush on a paper towel to remove excess paint. Hold the untaped side of the stencil in place with your fingers. Apply the paint with a pouncing or circular motion, working from the outside in, leaving the centre of the leaves lighter. Wipe the stencil clean between each use.

Wash the stencil after completing the leaves, and remove the tape covering the berries. Mask the top of the leaves near the berries with masking tape. Using red paint on the other stencil brush, stencil the berries, as above.

After finishing the border, place the cloth on the table and stencil three sets of leaves with berries at each corner. Randomly stencil sprigs of holly over the rest of the cloth. Allow to dry.

If using acrylic paint and fabric medium, iron the cloth to heat-set the cloth. If using fabric paint, follow the manufacturer's directions to fix the paint so that the cloth is washable.

Referring to the photograph below, stencil the napkins to match.

*This pretty holly-sprigged cloth started life as a single bedsheet, with the holly taken from the Christmas stencil on the cover.
We set up the table with a green undercloth first and the stencilled cloth on top.*

Stencil napkins to match — either cloth ones as below or purchased paper napkins.

China and crystal: Waterford Wedgwood. Candles: Illuminate

Crackers

Crackers almost fizzled out before they started when, in the mid-nineteenth century, English baker Tom Smith first had the idea of wrapping sweets in a twist of coloured paper — without the snap. To improve mediocre sales Smith inserted a small firecracker in each bonbon, with spectacular results.

Simple and fun to make, crackers can be fanciful, traditional, rustic or any style you please. Make them to match your chosen Christmas theme, and trim them with whatever you have on hand — we provide a few suggestions, along with jokes and gift ideas. We also give instructions for a set of boxed crackers that are almost too beautiful to pull.

BOXED CRACKERS

MATERIALS

For crackers:

Thin cardboard

Matt gold wrapping paper

**Thin handmade paper
(to wrap around gold paper)**

Deckle-edged scissors

Double-sided tape

Tissue paper, for paper hats

Craft glue

**Gifts and jokes
(see page 80 for suggestions)**

Snaps (from craft shops)

Raffia

For presentation box:

Corrugated cardboard

Spray adhesive

Two coordinating handmade papers

Craft knife or scissors

For trimming crackers and box:

White DAS

Biscuit cutters

Gold or raw sienna acrylic paint

Gold jewellery wire

**Dried leaves, cinnamon sticks,
cardamom pods, shells and other
natural objects**

Glue gun

CRACKERS

From cardboard, cut one rectangle, 10cm x 17cm, for inner tube, and two rectangles, each 4.5cm x 17cm, for outer ends. Roll each piece of card, overlapping 1.5cm, and secure with double-sided tape.

Using deckle-edged scissors, from matt gold paper, cut a rectangle, 36cm x 18cm. If using second layer, from handmade paper, cut a rectangle, 33cm x 18cm.

Place matt gold paper rectangle on a flat surface, wrong side up. Position inner tube roughly in centre of paper, then place a smaller tube on either side, with about 5cm in between. Secure tubes to paper with double-sided tape.

From tissue paper, make simple paper hats, using your own head for size. Insert paper hat, gift, joke and snap, securing the snap with a little double-sided tape.

Roll gold paper around tubes and secure with double-sided tape. If using a second layer, wrap handmade paper rectangle around tubes, allowing gold paper to protrude from ends, and secure with double-sided tape.

Gently squeeze crackers between tubes and tie with raffia, as tightly but as gently as possible.

Decorate as desired, using the glue gun to attach embellishments. To make DAS shapes, press DAS out thinly with palm of hand, cut out shapes using biscuit cutters, then allow to dry. Wash with gold or raw sienna paint. The jewellery wire has been coiled by hand.

JOKES

The tradition of including jokes in the crackers dates back to Tom Smith's early bonbons. The following jokes are corny enough to qualify as cracker material; they can be photocopied and inserted in your crackers, or you might have a few favourites of your own.

What do you call a deer with no eyes?
No idea.

Why did the man go outside with his wallet open?
He expected some change in the weather.

Why does lightning shock people?
Because it doesn't know how to conduct itself.

What do you call a boomerang that won't come back?
A stick.

What did the maths book say to the spelling book?
Boy, have I got problems.

What did Mrs Cook say when Captain Cook died?
"That's the way the Cookie crumbles."

Why do birds fly north?
Because it's too far for them to walk.

What do you get when you cross a blackbird with a mad dog?
A raven maniac.

How many men were born in 1900?
None, only babies were.

What did the mouse say when she got caught in the sewing machine?
"Well, I'll be darned."

How do you keep a silly person in suspense?
I'll tell you tomorrow.

When does a doctor get angry?
When she runs out of patients.

What do you get if you mix Aspirin with glue?
A cure for a splitting headache.

GIFT IDEAS

- *silver charm*
- *key ring*
- *thimble*
- *tiny pencil*
- *metal pencil sharpener*
- *decorative eraser*
- *bath cubes*
- *paste jewellery*
- *plastic insect*
- *assorted sweets*

PRESENTATION BOX

The presentation box is easy to make, so why not make two or three and use the spares as giftboxes?

Arrange crackers side by side and measure width and length to determine size of box base. Mark base rectangle on wrong side of corrugated card. Extend lines approximately 6cm at each corner, for box sides, then mark in larger rectangle to indicate tops of sides; cut around this line. Cut out squares formed at each corner, to make a cross shape. Score along foldlines of base, being careful not to cut through card, then fold up box sides and secure with tape. Make lid in the same way, remembering to add on approximately 5mm to the base measurements and to make the sides a little shorter.

Place box on wrong side of matt gold paper, trace around base, then extend lines at each corner for sides, adding on approximately 2cm for turnover. Mark in larger rectangle that indicates tops of sides and cut around this line. Cut along one of the lines going into each corner of base, leaving the other uncut. Spray wrong side of paper evenly with adhesive, then wrap around box, tucking under corners neatly. Repeat to cover box lid.

Decorate box lid as desired, using glue gun to attach ornaments. Our box has been embellished with a couple of squares of handmade paper, lengths of raffia, and a "raft" of cinnamon sticks with a piece of coiled jewellery wire and DAS heart on top. For a final touch, line the box with some deckle-edged handmade paper before arranging crackers inside.

TRIMMING SUGGESTIONS

✧ Use hand-stencilled or hand-painted paper to cover your crackers, and tie with a plain ribbon.

✧ Cover crackers with cream or white paper, then tie with gold cord and tassels, or with organza ribbon.

✧ Attach small tree ornaments to centre of cracker, using craft glue or glue gun.

✧ Personalise a cracker for each guest, by writing their name on a label and gluing it on.

✧ Decorate crackers with glittering dimensional paint, applied through squeeze-bottle applicators.

✧ Attach paper ribbons in bright colours.

There are dozens of simple ways to spruce up a cracker. The lovely old-fashioned look of these crêpe paper bonbons is achieved using motifs cut from Victoriana découpage paper, and scraps of this and that — tartan ribbon, lace and paper doilies ... anything that's lying around.

Christmas Stockings

Stockings are traditionally hung near the chimney in the hope that Santa will deposit small items in them on his way through. These brightly coloured stockings are sure to catch his eye as the perfect repositories for last-minute gifts and novelties.

APPLIQUÉ STOCKINGS

MEASUREMENTS

Each stocking is approximately 42cm long and 27cm wide from heel to toe.

MATERIALS

For one stocking:

Assortment of brightly coloured felts

0.3m x 115cm cotton print fabric

0.3m x 90cm paper-backed fusible webbing, such as Vliesofix

Stranded embroidery cotton in selection of bright colours

Size 7 crewel needle

Rickrack braid, bells, pompoms, large star sequins, string of brightly coloured beads, tiny beads, and other trims (optional: if making for a small child, add decorations in place of the bells and beads, which could be swallowed)

Note: *The photographed steps relate to the Ellie stocking.*

All patterns, including appliqué and embroidery outlines, for Merry Xmas stocking (front), Ellie stocking (front top, front centre and front toe), Ho Ho stocking (front top, front centre and front toe) and back stocking/front stocking lining are printed on the pattern sheet. Trace the desired patterns and appliqué outlines.

From contrasting coloured felts, cut one front stocking or required pieces for front stocking, one back stocking/front stocking lining, for back stocking, and required appliqué shapes (**Pic 1**).

From cotton print, cut one back stocking/front stocking lining, adding on 1cm seam allowance to top edge if making Merry Xmas stocking, for front stocking lining.

Here's Christmas cheer in plenty. Very few fabrics are as exuberantly coloured as felt — none is as simple to work.

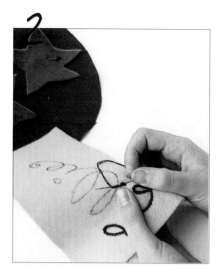

Position and pin appliqué shapes on the appropriate front stocking pieces — the stars and the sawtooth edging on the Ellie stocking, the pot and "Ho Ho" on the Ho Ho stocking, and the three layers of the star on the Merry Xmas stocking. Trace your chosen name onto the Ellie stocking, the tree on the Ho Ho stocking and greetings on the Merry Xmas stocking. Using six strands of contrasting embroidery cotton, embroider over marked lines in either chain stitch or backstitch (**Pic 2**).

Using two strands of embroidery cotton, blanket stitch or overstitch the appliqué shapes in place. Cut a piece of rickrack braid and, using one strand of contrasting embroidery cotton, secure the braid underneath the name on the Ellie stocking with hemming stitch. Add other embroidery or trims, as desired. For example, the tree on the Ho Ho stocking is adorned with a couple of felt hearts, each attached with a star sequin and a tiny bead.

Using six strands of contrasting embroidery thread, overstitch the three front pieces together to make up the front stocking (**Pic 3**). This step is not necessary if you are making the Merry Xmas stocking.

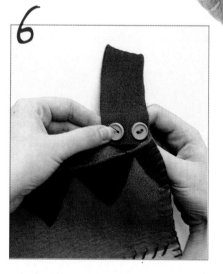

Press under 1cm along top edge of front lining. Place Vliesofix, paper side up, over wrong side of front stocking and trace around shape. Cut out stocking shape from Vliesofix, then place it, webbing side down, on wrong side of front stocking (**Pic 4**). Press to fuse. Peel off paper backing and press wrong side of front lining onto Vliesofix. There is no need to line back stocking.

With wrong sides facing, place front stocking on back stocking and trim away any excess so that both are the same size. Note that top edge of Ho Ho and Ellie stockings should sit slightly below top edge of back stocking to reveal coloured felt. Using wool or six strands of embroidery thread, blanket stitch the three layers together, starting at the top and working around the stocking (**Pic 5**).

Cut a hanging strip from felt and attach to the top right-hand corner of each stocking. We used brightly coloured buttons to attach the strip to the Ellie and Ho Ho stockings (**Pic 6**).

Turn down the front opening of the Merry Xmas stocking about 1cm to reveal the lining, and secure at intervals with large star sequins. Drape a string of baubles along the front opening of this stocking. Attach a bell or pompom to the toe of each stocking.

Sequins, spangles, stars and intentionally large and simple stitching all add charm to these easily made stockings. But don't feel impelled to follow these designs. The many other images of Christmas can all be adapted to suit these stockings.

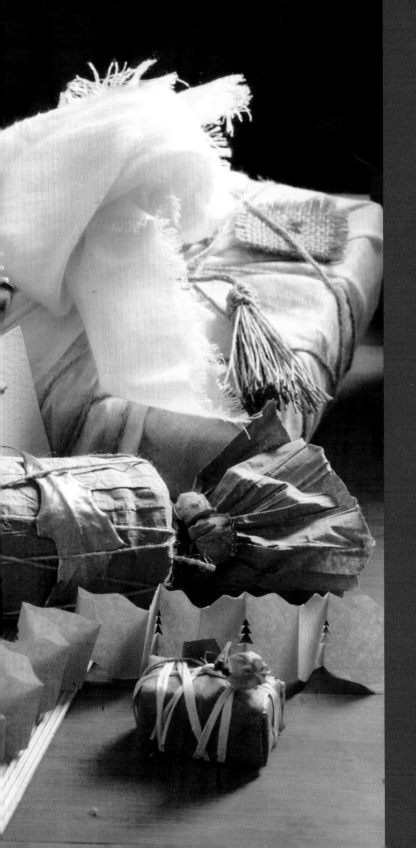

Cards and Wraps

The carefully chosen gift is only part of the gift-giving story; its presentation is just as important. But there's no need to spend a fortune on fancy wrappings and tags, as myriad imaginative ones can be created at home. And a handmade card is a gift in itself, lending a personal touch to what is now a very commercialised aspect of Christmas.

Trims and Tags

A quick rummage through the kitchen cupboards or a sortie into the garden can yield all the materials you need for original trims and tags. Make a pre-Christmas collection of objets trouvés *and recyclable materials, such as corrugated cardboard, hessian, lengths of string, seed pods and brown paper. Then simply use your imagination when combining bits and pieces. If you stick with a basic natural colour scheme, everything looks great together, despite its eclectic origins.*

TRIMS

Top left A variety of natural bric-a-brac, including dried grasses, seed pods, bark and a pretty shaped leaf, adds whimsical detail to naturally wrapped presents.

Top right Variations on the theme of corrugated cardboard and hessian will always look good; when combined, these materials form unusual and elegant trims.

Bottom left Glue or stitch star sequins to inexpensive sheer fabric, such as nylon curtaining, for a romantic, ethereal giftwrap, and add a star to a matching tag.

Bottom right For a Hollywood-style presentation, dress up star-studded giftwrap with a gold bow and a star tag cut from stencil plastic.

TAGS

Gold Leaf A coating of gold paint gives a pressed leaf the appearance of beaten metal.

3D Heart Use biscuit cutters to cut out simple DAS shapes, apply a thin gold or raw sienna wash, then attach to a natural tag using raffia or string.

Embossed Heart To emboss shapes, cut out the desired shape from thin card, place a second piece of textured paper over the shape and rub gently with a round-edged modelling tool.

Star Another DAS shape, this time simply glued to a piece of corrugated card.

Seed Pod and Wire Try mixing natural textured paper and seed pods with festive wire.

Pressed Leaf Press large leaves or petals between the pages of a phone book until they become paper-like; there's no need to do anything further except thread through a raffia tie.

Papers

Wrapping papers, gift boxes and bags, all with great style and personality, can be produced at home — and for a negligible cost. Adults and older kids can make original and elegant giftwrap by wielding a potato stamp or the stencil on the cover, while younger kids can do inventive things with spray bottles and food dye, drinking straws and dish-washing liquid.

stamps and stencils

STENCILLED GIFTWRAP AND CARRY BAGS

Using the cover stencil and inexpensive paper, you can create a sophisticated range of wrappings and tags. We spattered and stencilled— in a restrained fashion — onto litho paper, paper carry bags and papier-mâché boxes. Raffia and gold ribbon tied the theme in place. See page 74 for stencilling instructions.

POTATO STAMP WRAPPINGS

MATERIALS

Brown paper or litho paper
Papier-mâché box
Brick red and gold acrylic paints
Sponge roller
Paintbrush
Potato
Sharp kitchen knife
Biscuit cutter in star shape
Paper ribbon and raffia, or other trim materials

Using the sponge roller and the brick red paint, make an all-over checked pattern on the paper; don't worry about neatness (**Pic 1**). If decorating a papier-mâché box, use the paintbrush to apply paint over its entire surface.

Cut the potato in half. Use a biscuit cutter to impress a star pattern on the surface of one half, then cut away the excess around the edges of the star; the star shape should be about 3mm higher than its surrounds. Dip the raised star shape into undiluted gold paint, press the potato stamp onto the paper (anywhere you like), and remove carefully (**Pic 2**). Re-dip the stamp and repeat, until you've achieved a random pattern. Do the same for the box. Trim with paper ribbon and raffia, or as desired.

These no-fuss wrappings are easily created with the aid of a potato stamp and sponge roller, while the trims are quickly put together out of raffia and paper ribbon.

Fun for Kids

All of these activities are geared to the great outdoors, but they can be done inside if you don't mind a bit of mess and you've got newspaper on hand.

GENERAL MATERIALS

Butcher's paper or litho paper
Acrylic paint, ink and gouache in bright colours
Scissors
Craft glue
Lots of newspaper

TORN TISSUE PAPER

Tear different coloured tissue papers into any shape you like. Spread craft glue thinly on the tissue shapes, then glue them to a sheet of litho or butcher's paper in a random fashion, overlapping shapes and mixing the colours well.

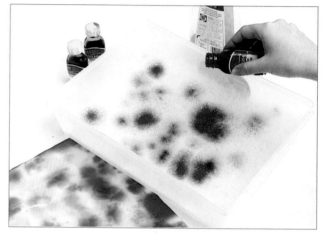

WASHING-UP LIQUID

A baking tray or flat Tupperware dish will come in handy for this activity. Trim your paper so that it fits neatly in the tray (but don't put it in yet). Pour water into the tray, and mix in some detergent — vigorously, so as to produce lots of bubbles. Drop different coloured inks into the froth, and lay your paper gently on top. Lift the paper out and allow to dry.

SPATTERING

An old toothbrush comes into its own here. Lay out sheets of paper ready for spattering, and mix powder paint with water in a saucer to a light, creamy consistency. Dip the toothbrush in the paint, and tap it over newspaper to remove excess paint. Hold it over the wrapping paper and run your finger down the bristles to give a fine spray of droplets all over the paper. When the paper is covered, change colours, washing the toothbrush well between colours, and repeat several times. You can achieve special effects by using leaves or other objects as masks, and spattering over the top of them.

BLOWN INK

For this effect, you will need a drinking straw as well as the general materials. Lay out litho or butcher's paper ready for spraying. In an eggcup, mix paint with water until you have a runny consistency. If using ink, there is no need to add water. Insert straw, suck *gently* and blow the paint or ink onto the paper. Allow to dry, then repeat with another colour. Stop when you are happy with the result. Do not overdo it, or you will lose the jewelled effect.

Starting from the left and working clockwise, there's torn tissue, blown ink, spattered paint, paint rolled with marbles and ink frothed up by washing-up liquid. Once you've wrapped up your gifts in these vibrant papers you'll want to add some imaginative trims, such as the lollipop and raffia one shown here.

MARBLES IN A TRAY

For this experiment, you'll need some marbles and a large baking tray (or you could cut down a cardboard box to form a tray). Trim the paper so that it lies snugly in the tray, then lay it on the bottom of the tray. Drop undiluted acrylic paint onto the surface of the paper to form blobs (don't make the blobs too big). Now, before the paint dries, drop some marbles onto the paper and allow them to roll over the surface, picking up bits of paint as they roll. The result will be colourful rather than neat.

Cards and Ties

Whether "Merry Christmas" is said with flowers or cut paper and ribbon, the recipients of the handcrafted card will appreciate the effort taken. So why not start on your Christmas list a bit earlier this year? As well as avoiding that horrible last-minute panic, you will have tremendous fun making your own cards. And, for the grand finale, we show you how to tie up the whole present-wrapping business with the perfect bow.

Ideas for Cards

ETCHED CARDS

MATERIALS

Cartridge paper

Yellow oxide acrylic paint

Flat fitch brush

White wax candle

Black ink

Wooden satay stick

Tan-coloured paper or card, for mount

White paper or card, for card backing

Pencil and ruler

Craft knife or scissors

Glue stick

Cut cartridge paper into card-sized pieces. Thin the yellow paint with water and, using the flat brush, paint wavy lines across each cartridge card. Allow to dry. Using the white candle, rub over the entire surface in all directions, pressing down quite hard so that you achieve a solid layer of wax all over the paper (**Pic 1**).

Brush black ink all over the surface (**Pic 2**).

To mount your card, glue the design onto a piece of tan card or paper cut slightly larger than the design (use deckle-edged scissors to cut tan paper if you wish). Measure and cut a two-panel mount from the white paper or card, with each panel slightly larger than the tan mount, and fold into a card shape. Glue the mounted design onto the front of the folded white mount.

When the ink is dry, use either end of the satay stick to scratch a design into the ink to reveal the yellow and white areas (**Pic 3**). See the photograph below for design ideas.

STAINED GLASS CARDS

MATERIALS

Stiff black paper or thin black card
Pencil and ruler
Scissors
Tracing paper
Red, blue, yellow and
**   green pieces of cellophane**
Craft knife
Cotton bud
Glue stick
White paper or card

Three designs are included on the pattern sheet. Measure and cut a black three-panel mount, with each panel the same size as the outline of your chosen design. Fold mount into three.

Trace your chosen design onto the inside of the centre panel in pencil (**Pic 1**). Use a craft knife to cut out the shaded shapes, being careful not to cut the strips in between.

Cut out different-coloured cellophane shapes to match the cut-out areas. Use a cotton bud to apply glue from the glue stick around the edges of the cut-out areas and stick cellophane shapes in place (**Pic 2**).

Cut a piece of white paper or card slightly larger than the window and glue it behind the cellophane (**Pic 3**).

Fold the front flap of the black mount over the white card and glue in place.

PRESSED FLOWER CARDS
MATERIALS

Leaves and flowers for pressing
**Microfleur flower press or old phone
  books**
Gold spray paint
Stiff paper or thin card
Craft knife
Scissors
Cotton bud
Glue stick
**Gold stars, ribbon and fabric scraps,
  for decoration**

*Choose flowers or leaves that
suggest a Christmas image or
arrange pressed flowers into a
seasonal motif. Here, sweet
Alice, or alyssum, forms a
golden wreath, while love-in-
the-mist looks festive on its own,
and clover flowers are artfully
arranged into the shape of a
Christmas tree.*

Use only undamaged flowers or leaves for pressing; tatty specimens will not look any better
when pressed. It is also best to press flowers when
they are dry, as wet flowers will go mouldy during the pressing process.

   To speed up the pressing process, we used a
Microfleur flower press and a microwave oven.
Place one of the Microfleur platens, ribbed side
down, on a bench, place one pad on top and
then one piece of fabric on top of the pad. Place
the specimens to be pressed on the fabric sheet,
making sure they lie flat and do not overlap or
touch each other (**Pic 1**). Place the second fabric
sheet, pad and platen (ribbed side up) on top of
the specimens. Apply a little pressure to the top
platen while you slide the two clips in place on
opposite sides of the platen. The Microfleur is
now ready to go in the microwave. Specimens
should be dried in bursts. As a guideline, the initial burst should be about 45 seconds for a 600W
oven, 30 seconds for a 750W oven and 20 seconds
for a 900W oven. Secondary bursts should be
about one-half to one-third of the initial burst.
If specimens are particularly dry when put in the
Microfleur, reduce the initial burst time by half.

   If you haven't got a Microfleur, the pressing
process is more leisurely. At least six weeks before
you wish to make the cards, simply place the flowers or leaves within the pages of an old telephone
book, and place another phone book on top. Leave
alone (no peeking) for six weeks.

   Once you have your pressed specimens, place
on a sheet of newspaper and spray with metallic
paint (**Pic 2**). Allow to dry.

Glue the sprayed flowers or leaves on a card, in
desired arrangement, and add trims as desired.
Here we chose a fern frond that has a Christmas
tree shape and so required no further work; we
simply added a star at its apex (**Pic 3**).

   Smaller pressed flowers can be arranged into
a Christmas image, or gold or silver flowers and
leaves can be simply glued to a card in a pleas-
ing arrangement. The main photograph, above,
will give you some ideas.

RIBBON CARDS

MATERIALS

Textured handmade paper
Pencil
Metal ruler
Scalpel
Cutting mat
Thin coloured card, for mounting
Wide organza ribbon
Gold stars (optional)
Glue stick
Card studs

These fanciful cards are easy to re-create: simply thread organza ribbon through cuts made in handmade paper, then scrunch and pull the loops for a textural effect. Look for ribbon printed with festive images — we used star-patterned organza — to convey your season's greetings.

Measure and cut a piece of handmade paper that is about 2cm wider than the width of the ribbon and about 12cm long. Mark parallel lines across the handmade paper piece, starting and finishing each line approximately 1cm from side of paper; the distance between the lines alternates between 5mm and 1cm and you will need an even number of lines. Using a metal ruler and scalpel, and working on a cutting mat, cut along the marked lines (**Pic 1**).

Cut a length of ribbon approximately three times the length of the handmade paper piece. Take one end down through the first cut in the handmade paper, leaving a tail of about 10cm. Bring the ribbon up through the second cut and take it down through the third, pulling gently so as to leave a loop on the right side of the paper. Continue threading the ribbon through the cuts in this manner, leaving loops and bringing the ribbon up through the last cut. Adjust loops to make them even (**Pic 2**). Trim one end of the ribbon in a curve and cut a "V" shape in the other end to prevent fraying.

Measure and cut a two-panel mount from the coloured card, with the front panel of the mount about 2cm larger all round than the handmade paper piece. Fold into a card shape. Glue the threaded ribbon piece onto the front of the folded mount. Using a card stud, secure each end of the ribbon (**Pic 3**). Decorate the finished card with gold stars, if desired. See the main photograph, above, for other ways of using threaded ribbon.

The Perfect Bow

HAND-TIED BOW

CENTRE-TIED BOW

1

From one ribbon, cut a length more than five times the finished width of the bow, and cut ends in a "V" shape to prevent fraying. Make several loops in this ribbon length (**Pic 1**).

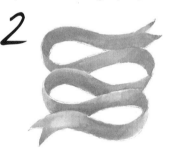

2

From a second ribbon, cut a length a little less than five times the finished width of the bow, and cut a "V" shape in the ends. Make several smaller loops in this length (**Pic 2**).

1

Cut ribbon approximately four times the width of the finished bow and trim the ends in a "V" shape to prevent fraying. Make two loops in the ribbon, holding one in each hand (**Pic 1**).

1

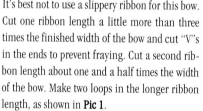

It's best not to use a slippery ribbon for this bow. Cut one ribbon length a little more than three times the finished width of the bow and cut "V"s in the ends to prevent fraying. Cut a second ribbon length about one and a half times the width of the bow. Make two loops in the longer ribbon length, as shown in **Pic 1**.

2

Fold the right loop over and then under the left, and through the loop (**Pic 2**), then pull the bow firmly and arrange into desired shape.

2

Use the shorter ribbon length to bind the centre (**Pic 2**). You will need to ease the ribbon end at the front to the back of the bow.

3

Lay the second looped length on the first one, and bind with another piece of ribbon (**Pic 3**).

Pompom Bow

Bind a double bow with ribbon, and tuck in natural trims such as gold-sprayed seed pods and leaves.

1

This bow requires approximately 3.5m of ribbon. Make a loop in the end of the ribbon about 20cm across, then wrap the ribbon around about 10 times (**Pic 1**).

2

Flatten the loops and cut off triangles at each end (**Pic 2**).

Raffia and rustic-looking paper roses or dried flowers add texture to paper bows.

3

Bring the ends together in the middle, matching the cut triangles (**Pic 3**). Wrap the centre with wire, and tease out loops, twisting them as you turn.

For an added sparkle, wrap a starry wire around a multicoloured pompom bow.

Carols

Whether it's Carols by Candle-light under a warm southern sky or a lamplit impromptu choir on a cold and frosty evening, carol singing gives us a chance to sing with joy. Here is a selection of all the favourites. You'll be familiar with most of them, but we've provided melody lines just in case ... so that you can raise your voices wherever you are.

Away in a Manger

G

A - way in a___ man - ger, no___ crib for a bed, The___

Am   D7   G   A7   D7

lit - tle Lord Je - sus laid___ down His sweet head. The

G   G7   C

stars in the___ bright sky looked___ down where He lay, The___

D7   G   D7   G

lit - tle Lord Je - sus a - sleep on the hay.

The cattle are lowing, the Baby awakes,
But little Lord Jesus no crying He makes.
I love Thee, Lord Jesus!
    Look down from the sky,
And stay by my side until morning is nigh.

Be near me, Lord Jesus; I ask Thee to stay
Close by me forever, and love me I pray.
Bless all the dear children in Thy tender care,
And fit us for Heaven, to live with Thee there.

While Shepherds Watched

F   C   F   Bb   F   C

While shep - herds watched their flocks by night, All

F   G7   C   F   Bb

seat - ed on the ground, The an - gel of the

C   Dm   A7   Bb   C7   F

Lord came down, And glo - ry shone a - round.

"Fear not," said he (for mighty dread
Had seized their troubled mind);
"Glad tidings of great joy I bring
To you, and all mankind.

"To you in David's town this day
Is born of David's line
A Saviour, who is Christ the Lord;
And this shall be the sign:
The heavenly babe you there shall find
To human view displayed,
All meanly wrapped in swathing bands,
And in a manger laid."

Thus spake the seraph: and forthwith
Appeared a shining throng
Of angels praising God, who thus
Addressed their joyful song:
"All glory be to God on high,
And to the earth be peace;
Goodwill henceforth from heaven to men
Begin, and never cease."

Once in Royal David's City

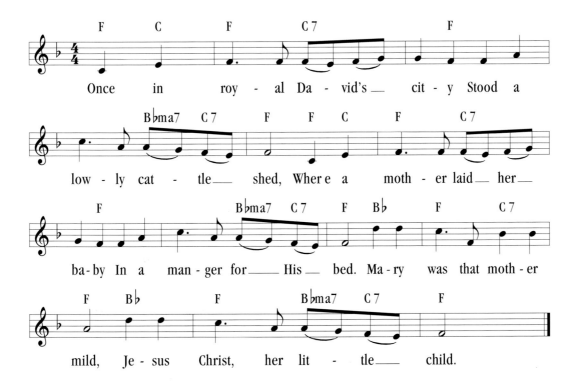

Once in roy - al Da - vid's cit - y Stood a low - ly cat - tle shed, Where a moth - er laid her ba - by In a man - ger for His bed. Ma - ry was that moth - er mild, Je - sus Christ, her lit - tle child.

He came down to earth from heaven,
Who is God and Lord of all,
And his shelter was a stable,
And his cradle was a stall,
With the poor, and mean, and lowly,
Lived on earth our Saviour holy.

And through all his wondrous childhood,
He would honour and obey,
Love and watch the lowly mother
In whose gentle arms he lay.
Christian children all must be
Mild, obedient, good as he.

And our eyes at last shall see him,
Through his own redeeming love
For that child so dear and gentle
Is our Lord in heaven above;
And he leads his children on
To the place where he has gone.

Hark! The Herald Angels Sing

Hark! the her-ald an-gels sing,— "Glo-ry to the new-born King.

Peace on earth and mer-cy mild,— God and sin-ners re-con-ciled!"

Joy-ful, all ye na-tions rise,— Join the tri-umph of the skies;—

With th'an-gel-ic host pro-claim, "Christ is—born in Beth-le-hem!"

Hark! the her-ald an-gels sing, "Glo-ry— to the new-born King."

Christ, by highest heaven adored,
Christ, the everlasting Lord,
Late in time behold Him come
Offspring of the Virgin's womb;
Veiled in flesh the Godhead see;
Hail the incarnate Deity!
Pleased as man with man to dwell,
Jesus, our Emmanuel.

Chorus
Hark! the herald angels sing,
Glory to the new-born King.

Hail the heaven-born Prince of Peace!
Hail the Sun of Righteousness!
Light and life to all He brings,
Risen with healing in His wings.
Mild He lays His glory by,
Born that man no more may die,
Born to raise the sons of earth,
Born to give them second birth.

Chorus

The First Noel

The — first — No - el the — an - gel did say Was to
cer - tain poor shep - herds in fields as they lay; In —
fields — where — they lay — keep - ing their sheep On a
cold win - ter's night — that was — so deep.
No - el, — No - el, No - el, No - el,
Born is the King — of Is - ra - el.

They looked up and saw a star,
Shining in the East beyond them far,
And to the earth it gave great light,
And so it continued both day and night.

Chorus
Noel, Noel, Noel, Noel,
Born is the King of Israel.

And by the light of that same star,
Three wise men came from country far;
To seek for a King was their intent,
And to follow the star wherever it went.

Chorus

This star drew nigh to the north-west,
O'er Bethlehem it took its rest,
And there it did stop and stay,
Right over the place where Jesus lay.

Chorus

Then entered in those wise men three
Fell reverently upon their knee,
And offered there, in His presence,
Their gold, and myrrh, and
    frankincense.

Chorus

Then let us all with one accord
Sing praises to our heavenly Lord,
That hath made heaven and earth of
    nought,
And with His blood mankind hath
    bought.

Chorus

We Three Kings of Orient Are

We three Kings of O-ri-ent are; Bear-ing
gifts we tra-verse a - far. Field and foun - tain,
moor and moun - tain, fol - low - ing yon - der star.
O____ Star of won - der, star of night, Star with
roy - al beau - ty bright; West-ward lead - ing, still pro -
ceed - ing, Guide us to thy per - fect light.

Born a King on Bethlehem's plain;
Gold I bring to crown him again.
King forever, ceasing never,
Over us all to reign.

Chorus
Star of wonder, star of night,
Star with royal beauty bright;
Westward leading, still proceeding,
Guide us to thy perfect light.

Frankincense to offer have I;
Incense owns a Deity nigh.
Prayer and praising, all men raising,
Worship him God most high.

Chorus

Myrrh is mine; its bitter perfume;
Breathes a life of gathering gloom.
Sorrowing, sighing, bleeding, dying,
Sealed in the stone cold tomb.

Chorus

Glorious now behold him arise;
King and God and Sacrifice.
Alleluia, Alleluia,
Earth to heaven replies.

Chorus

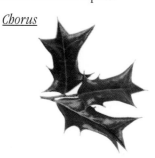

O Come, All Ye Faithful

O come, all ye faith - ful, Joy - ful and tri - um - phant, O
come ye, O come — ye to Beth - le - hem;
Come and be - hold Him, Born the King of an - gels:
O come, let us a - dore Him, O come, let us a - dore Him, O
come, let us a - dore Him, — Christ — the Lord.

Sing, choirs of angels
Sing in exultation
Sing, all ye citizens of heaven above,
Glory to God
In the highest:

Chorus
O come, let us adore Him,
O come, let us adore Him,
O come, let us adore Him,
   Christ the Lord.

Yea, Lord, we greet Thee,
Born this happy morning;
Jesus, to Thee be glory given,
Word of the Father,
Now in flesh appearing:

Chorus

Silent Night

Si - lent night, ho - ly night! All is calm,

all is bright. Round yon Vir - gin Moth - er and Child.

Ho - ly In - fant, so ten - der and mild, Sleep in heav - en - ly

peace,_____ Sleep __ in heav - en - ly peace! _____

Silent night, holy night!
Shepherds first saw the light,
Heard resounding clear and long
Far and near the angel song;
Christ the Saviour is here,
Christ the Saviour is here.

Silent night, holy night!
Son of God, oh how bright
Love is smiling from Thy face
Peals for us the hour of grace:
Christ our Saviour is born,
Christ our Saviour is born.

I saw Three ships

I saw three ships come sail - ing by, On

Christ - mas Day, on Christ - mas Day, I saw three ships come

sail - ing by, On Christ - mas Day in the morn - ing.

And who was in those ships all three,
On Christmas Day, on Christmas Day,
And who was in those ships all three,
On Christmas Day in the morning?

Our Saviour Christ and His Lady,
On Christmas Day, on Christmas Day,
Our Saviour Christ and His Lady,
On Christmas Day in the morning.

Oh! they sailed into Bethlehem,
On Christmas Day, on Christmas Day,
Oh! they sailed into Bethlehem,
On Christmas Day in the morning.

And all the bells on earth shall ring,
On Christmas Day, on Christmas Day,
And all the bells on earth shall ring,
On Christmas Day in the morning.

And all the Angels in Heaven shall sing,
On Christmas Day, on Christmas Day,
And all the Angels in Heaven shall sing,
On Christmas Day in the morning.

And all the souls on earth shall sing,
On Christmas Day, on Christmas Day,
And all the souls on earth shall sing,
On Christmas Day in the morning.

O Christmas Tree

O Christmas tree, O Christmas tree
Much pleasure doth thou bring me!
O Christmas tree, O Christmas tree
Much pleasure doth thou bring me!

For every year the Christmas tree,
Bring to us all both joy and glee
O Christmas tree, O Christmas tree
Much pleasure doth thou bring me!

O Christmas tree, O Christmas tree,
Thy candles shine out brightly!
O Christmas tree, O Christmas tree,
Thy candles shine out brightly!

Each bough doth hold its tiny light,
That makes each toy to sparkle bright.
O Christmas tree, O Christmas tree,
Thy candles shine out brightly!

Ding Dong Merrily on High

Ding dong mer-ri-ly on high! In heav'n the bells are ring-ing.

Ding dong ve-ri-ly the sky Is riv'n with an-gels sing-ing:

Glo - - - - - - - - - - - -

- - - - - ri - a, Ho-san-na in ex-cel-sis!

E'en so here below, below
Let steeple bells be swungen
And i-o, i-o, i-o
By priest and people be sungen
Gloria, Hosanna in excelsis

Pray ye dutifully prime
Your matin chime, ye ringers
May ye beautifully rime
Your evetime song, ye singers
Gloria, Hosanna in excelsis

Jingle Bells

Jin - gle bells! Jin - gle bells! Jin - gle all the way!

Oh, what fun it is to ride in a one-horse o-pen sleigh! Hey!

Jin - gle bells! Jin - gle bells! Jin - gle all the way!

Oh, what fun it is to ride in a one-horse o-pen sleigh!

Dashing through the snow, in a one-
horse open sleigh,
O'er the fields we go, laughing all the
way.

Bells on bobtails ring, making spirits
bright,
What fun it is to ride and sing a sleighing
song tonight.

Repeat first verse

It Came Upon a Midnight Clear

It came up-on the mid-night clear, That glo-rious song of
old, From an-gels bend-ing near the earth To
touch their harps of gold: "Peace on the earth, goodwill to men, From heav'n's all gra-cious King!" The
world in sol-emn still-ness lay To hear the an-gels sing.

Still through the cloven skies they come,
With peaceful wings unfurled,
And still their heavenly music floats
O'er all the weary world:
Above its sad and lowly pains
They bend on hovering wing,
And ever o'er its Babel sounds
The blessed angels sing.

For lo! The days are hastening on,
By prophet bards foretold,
When with the ever-circling years
Comes round the age of gold;
When peace shall over all the earth
Its ancient splendours fling,
And the whole world send back the song
Which now the angels sing.

Deck the Halls

Deck the halls with boughs of hol-ly, Fa la la la la la la la la!

'Tis the sea-son to be jol-ly, Fa la la la la la la la la!

Don we now our gay ap-par-el, Fa la la la la la la la la!

Sing the an-cient Yule-tide car-ol, Fa la la la la la la la la!

See the blazing Yule before us,
Fa la la la la la la la la.
Strike the harp and join the chorus,
Fa la la la la la la la la.
Follow me in merry measure,
Fa la la la la la la la la.
While I tell of Yuletide treasure,
Fa la la la la la la la la.

Fast away the old year passes,
Fa la la la la la la la la.
Fail the new ye lads and lasses,
Fa la la la la la la la la.
Sing we joyous altogether,
Fa la la la la la la la la.
Heedless of the wind and weather,
Fa la la la la la la la la.

Joy to the World

Joy to the world! the Lord is come; Let earth re-

ceive her King! Let ev-'ry heart prepare Him

room, And heav'n and na-ture sing, And heav'n and na-ture

sing, And heav'n and heav'n and na-ture sing.

Joy to the earth! The Savior reigns;
Let men their songs employ;
While fields and floods
Rocks, hills and plains
Repeat the sounding joy,
Repeat the sounding joy,
Repeat, repeat the sounding joy.

No more let sins and sorrows grow,
Nor thorns infest the ground;
He comes to make His blessing flow
Far as the curse is found,
Far as the curse is found,
Far as, far as the curse is found.

He rules the world with truth and grace,
And makes the nations prove
The glories of His righteousness,
And wonders of His love,
And wonders of His love,
And wonders, wonders of His love.

The Holly and the Ivy

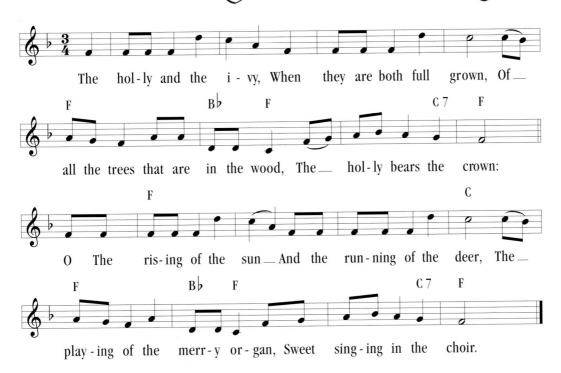

The hol-ly and the i-vy, When they are both full grown, Of all the trees that are in the wood, The hol-ly bears the crown: O The ris-ing of the sun And the run-ning of the deer, The play-ing of the merr-y or-gan, Sweet sing-ing in the choir.

The holly bears a blossom,
As white as the lily flower,
And Mary bore sweet Jesus Christ,
To be our sweet Saviour:

Chorus
The rising of the sun
And the running of the deer,
The playing of the merry organ,
Sweet singing in the choir.

The holly bears a berry,
As red as any blood,
And Mary bore sweet Jesus Christ,
To do poor sinners good:

Chorus

The holly bears a prickle,
As sharp as any thorn,
And Mary bore sweet Jesus Christ
On Christmas day in the morn:

Chorus

The holly bears a bark,
As bitter as any gall,
And Mary bore sweet Jesus Christ
For to redeem us all:

Chorus

Good King Wenceslas

Good King Wen-ces-las looked out   On the Feast of   Ste - phen,

When the snow lay 'round a-bout,   Deep and crisp and   e - ven;

Bright - ly shone the   moon that night,   Though the   frost   was

cru - el,   When   a   poor   man   came   in   sight,

Gath - 'ring   win - ter   fu - - - el.

"Hither, page, and stand by me,
If thou know'st it, telling.
Yonder peasant, who is he?
Where and what his dwelling?
"Sire, he lives a good league hence,
Underneath the mountain,
Right against the forest fence,
By Saint Agnes' fountain."

"Bring me flesh and bring me wine,
Bring me pine logs hither:
Thou and I wilt see him dine,
When we bear them thither."
Page and monarch forth they went,
Forth they went together;
Through the rude wind's wild lament,
And the bitter weather.

"Sire, the night is darker now,
And the wind blows stronger;
Fails my heart, I know not how;
I can go no longer."
"Mark my footsteps, my good page;
Tread thou in them boldly:
Thou shalt find the winter's rage
Freeze thy blood less coldly."

In his master's steps he trod,
Where the snow lay dinted;
Heat was in the very sod
Which the saint had printed.
Therefore, Christian men, be sure,
Wealth or rank possessing,
Ye who now will bless the poor,
Shall yourselves find blessing.

We Wish You a Merry Christmas

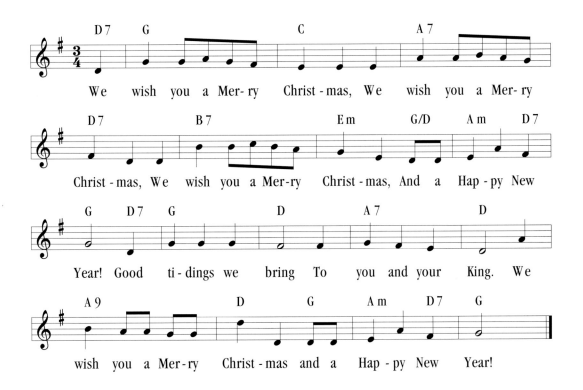

We wish you a Merry Christ-mas, We wish you a Mer-ry Christ-mas, We wish you a Mer-ry Christ-mas, And a Hap-py New Year! Good ti-dings we bring To you and your King. We wish you a Mer-ry Christ-mas and a Hap-py New Year!

We all want some figgy pudding,
We all want some figgy pudding,
We all want some figgy pudding, so
   bring some out here!

Chorus
Good tidings we bring to you and
   your King.
We wish you a merry Christmas and a
happy New Year.

We won't go until we get some,
We won't go until we get some,
We won't go until we get some, so
   bring some out here!

Chorus

We wish you a merry Christmas,
We wish you a merry Christmas,
We wish you a merry Christmas and a
   happy New Year.

Fun
and Games

As the afternoon wears on, and
the effects of the Christmas
dinner wear off, guests could
be in the mood for some fun
and games. They might not be
up to performing a full-scale
pantomime, which is the
traditional Christmas entertainment, but they might be
energetic enough for charades,
which are also customary — or
one of the many other, less
theatrical, family games.

Christmas Entertainments

Here's your chance to entertain or be entertained, to ham it up or let your hair down ... in other words, to enjoy some old-fashioned all-in family fun.

When I Looked in My Stocking

This is a word game in which each player takes it in turn to state an item found in a Christmas stocking. As the game progresses the recited list becomes longer and longer and must be repeated by each player before he or she adds the next item. For example, the first player might say, "When I looked in my stocking this morning I found a yellow beach umbrella." The second player then repeats this and adds to it: "When I looked in my stocking this morning I found a yellow beach umbrella and bright pink underpants." And so to the third player, who adds their contribution. The game works its way back to the first player, and continues until someone forgets a present or puts one in the wrong order and is thus out. The last player left in is the winner.

Charades

Traditionally, charades is a game for two teams. One team leaves the scene and thinks of a word that divides neatly into syllables that are words on their own; for example, "cut-let". The team comes back and announces how many syllables the word has and then acts out a scene for the word "cut". The team members go out again and return to act out another scene for the word "let". They leave again and return to act out a third scene for the whole word, "cutlet". The audience then has three guesses at the whole word. Whether they are right or not, they take the next turn acting out a word.

Some good words to try include:

forbid (four/bid)

dinosaur (dine/no/saw)

illusion (ill/ewe/shone)

artichoke (art/tea/choke)

populate (pop/you/late)

fortunate (four/tune/ate)

puritan (pure/I/tan)

childhood (child/hood)

tolerate (toll/err/rate)

Less traditionally, the game can be played with a single person acting out, syllable by syllable, a word or a phrase, or the title of a book, play, film, song, TV or radio program in a series of silent but inventive mimes.

Happy Christmas

Players count aloud in turn until the number 5 is reached. The words "Happy Christmas" must be substituted for 5 and thereafter for any multiple of 5 (15, 20 etc.). A player who fails to do so is out. Once everyone has mastered this, make it harder. For example, 7 and multiples of 7 (14, 21 etc.) can be replaced by the words "Joyful New Year". Multiples of both 5 and 7 (35, 70 etc.) are replaced by "Happy Christmas and a Joyful New Year". If you reach 70, you are mathematical geniuses.

The Song Game

The person beginning the game gives a word from a song — for example "blue" — and then sings the line with that word in it. The second person sings a line from a different song with the nominated word in it, and so on around the room back to the first person, who takes a second turn.

The player on the first person's left then starts a new round with a different word. Anyone who can't think of a song is out; the winner is the last person left in.

Songs with the word "blue" in them could include "Blue Moon", and "Blue Suede Shoes" (though the word doesn't have to be in the title). Other words are "wish" ("I Wish I Were a Rich Man", "When You Wish Upon a Star") and "night" ("Here Comes the Night", "Tonight's the Night").

Recitation

A traditional Christmas entertainment from the days before television (and radio) was the reading aloud of Christmas stories and verses. Ghost stories, Victorian melodramas in verse, and horror tales were particularly popular. Try your local library for special Christmas collections or your own bookshelves, which might contain some of the following stories and verse:

"A Christmas Carol"
by Charles Dickens

"T'was the Night Before Christmas"
by Clement Clarke Moore

"The Fire at Ross's Farm"
by Henry Lawson

"Christmas Underground"
from *The Wind in the Willows*
by Kenneth Graham

Hunt the Thimble

You could play this with as few as two people, but the more the merrier. The game is simple: Everyone leaves the room except for one person, who "hides" a thimble or similar object. It must not be covered or placed underneath anything, but should be in "plain" view.

The others return to the room, and as each person spots the thimble he or she sits down, without giving the hiding place away.

The games continues until everyone has seen the thimble; the person who saw it first could then hide it again for the next round.

Index